THE ABCs

of

Italian Travel

Handwritten by

Danielle DiPietro Hawkins

An exploration of applicable words and phrases, nouns, and verbs utilizing each letter of the alphabet.

Published by Mindstir Media, LLC
45 Lafayette Rd | Suite 181| North Hampton, NH 03862 | USA
1.800.767.0531 | www.mindstirmedia.com

Printed in the United States of America
ISBN-13: 978-1-7327049-8-5
Library of Congress Control Number: 2018912512

MINDSTIR MEDIA

Benvenuti, amici! (Welcome, friends!)

Thank you (Grazie!) for purchasing my book! At the time of publishing, I have been teaching Italian at the college level, as well as privately, for 17 years. In recent years, there's been a decline in enrollment in my university transferrable classes, and an increase in students wanting to learn Italian for travel purposes. Because of this, I created a YouTube channel (Learn Italian for Travel) and a website: **www.learnitalianfortravel.com**. I recommend that along with studying this book, you also watch my videos so that you can hear the correct pronunciation.

I applaud you for studying Italian before you travel to Italy! It shows respect for the people and culture, and I guarantee it will make your travel experience more pleasurable. You can, of course, utilize this book even if you're not planning a trip to Italy. The first section is an in depth explanation of the grammatical concepts important for understanding the language. After the grammar, comes the alphabet. For each letter, I give applicable words and phrases, nouns, and verbs that you'll use while traveling. You'll notice that there is no J, K, W, X or Y, because these letters aren't included in the Italian alphabet.

I wrote this book by hand because I want you, the reader, to feel like this is a personal and easily integrated learning process. I want you to be relaxed as you study this beautiful language. This book is a compilation of my experience as an Italian teacher, as well as learner- living in Italy for a study abroad program, and other trips for pleasure. I hope that you enjoy yourself as much as I have! Buono studio! (Enjoy studying!)

Danielle

My Nonno, Enzo DiPietro, was born in a small Tuscan town called Bozzano on October 3, 1920. He immigrated to the United States when he was 9 years old, and later became an American soldier who fought in World War II.

During the war, he was stationed in Luxembourg, where he met his future wife, Odette Giannoni, who was also Italian. They fell in love .. he returned to the U.S. after the war was over, then went back to Luxembourg so they could get married. Together they created a life in the U.S. and a beautiful family with 4 sons, 8 grandchildren, and 10 great grandchildren.

They were married for 71 years.

My grandparents have always exemplified tenacity and strength of spirit. Their love for each other and appreciation of life's simple pleasures like family, good food and laughter has become foundational for me. They are the reason I learned to speak Italian ; to connect with my heritage and, in turn myself, in a more profound way. I will forever be grateful.

This year on January 31, 2018, my Nonno passed away. This book is for him.

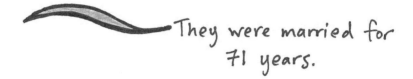

Mille grazie to my marvelous team of editors, Gina Lefebvre, Robert Quist, and Francesco Madaro.

Gina, whose impeccable knowledge of English grammar was quintessential.. Robert, whose bilingual skills served in both English and Italian corrections.. and Francesco, whose native Italian knowledge provided insight and depth.

Also, a huge thanks to 13 year old prodigious artist, Lola Parks, for providing the exceptional illustrations.

Cominciamo!

(Let's begin!)

Pronunciation

The Italian vowels make the following sounds:

a (ah)   **e** (ay) (eh)   **i** (ee)   **o** (open oh) (closed oh)   **u** (ooh)

Most words end in a vowel, and most words are accented on the second to last syllable. Some words have written accents on the last vowel, and some words defy the rule, and are accented on a different syllable:

ragazza (the norm)   **città** (written accent)   **àbito** (an exception)

There are only 2 written accents:

→ grave = this accent doesn't change the sound of the
(more common)   vowel ⟶ è (tè)

→ acute = this accent gives the vowel a more closed sound
(less common)   ⟶ é (perché)

There is no `ct` or `pt` combination in Italian. It will be replaced by `tt`:

October → ottobre
september → settembre

- `x` will be replaced by `s`
- `j` will be replaced by `g`
- `y` will be replaced by `i` or another vowel combination.

When 'c' and 'g' are followed by 'e' or 'i', they make the following sounds:

cena = chay·nah
cinque = cheen·kway

('ch', like in 'church')

giro = jee·roh
gelato = jeh·lah·toh

('j', like in 'jelly')

When 'c' and 'g' are followed by 'a', 'o', 'u' or 'h', the sound is hard:

chi = kee
cosa = koh·zah

('k' like in 'key')

gamba = gahm·bah
gusto = goo·stoh

('g', like in 'gum')

When 'sc' is followed by 'e' or 'i' it makes a 'sh' sound like in 'shoe':

- scena = shay·nah
- sci = shee

And when it's followed by 'a', 'o', 'u' or 'h', the sound of the 'c' is hard as in 'school':

- scala = skah·lah
- scomodo = skoh·moh·doh
- schiena = skee·eh·nah

When 's' is in between 2 vowels, it has a hard 'z' sound :

    Pisa = Pee·zah
    casa = cah·zah

At the beginning of a word, or in between a vowel and a consonant, the 's' has a soft sound :

    Sorella = soh·reh·lah
    insalata = een·sah·lah·tah

The letter 'z' has 2 sounds :
   'ts' in the middle of a word → pizza = pee·tsah
or 'dz' in the beginning of a word → zona = dzoh·nah

The 'gn' combination sounds like the 'ny' in the word `canyon` :

    → gnocchi = nyoh·kee

The 'gl' combination can have an enunciated or a blended sound :

- gloria = gloh·ree·ah (enunciated)
- figlia = fee·lee·ah (blended)

See letter `g` for a better explanation on forming these sounds.

vi

The `ia` and `io` combination both have a blended or enunciated sound:

- spiaggia (contains both sounds)

  =

  spee·ah·jah (blended)
  (↗enunciated)
- farmacia = far·mah·chee·ah (enunciated)

All shops in the city that end in -ia have an enunciated -ia (ee·ah) sound.

- gioco = joh·koh (blended)
- scio = shee·oh (enunciated)

These vowel combinations make the following blended sounds:

ae = ah·ay
iu = ee·ooh
ai = ah·ee
ao = ah·oh
au = ah·ooh
ei = ay·ee

When you see a double consonant, rest slightly longer on that consonant sound, for it can change the meaning of the word ↪ (e.g. sette vs. sete)

Watch my YouTube video on pronunciation for practice!

Italia

Italy is a peninsula surrounded by various seas ('mare'), with Rome as its capital. It is divided into 20 regions, including 2 islands: Sicily and Sardinia. Each region has noteworthy differences, primarily in dialect and cuisine. There is an English translation for most of the region and city names (e.g. Toscana → Tuscany, Venezia → Venice).

Table of Contents

Each letter of the alphabet is organized into 'words and phrases', 'nouns' and 'verbs'. All of the verbs will be included in the table of contents, but only a few of the more important terms from the 'words and 'phrases' and 'nouns' sections.

The letters

✗

Subject Pronouns

io = I

tu = you (singular, informal)

lui = he

lei = she

Lei = you (singular, formal)

noi = we

voi = you (plural)

loro = they

The pronouns for she (lei) and you; formal (Lei) are the same. When written, the latter is distinguished with a capital. Use the formal pronoun 'Lei' when speaking to someone you have just met or don't know well. In contrast, use the 'tu' pronoun when speaking to someone with whom you are well acquainted. (e.g. family, friends, peers)

The subject pronouns are the foundation for conjugating a verb, as you will see in the following pages. Most of the time they will be associated with a verb, but you can also use them alone. For example, if someone asks you a question and you wish to ask the same question in return, simply say, 'And you?'

> Come sta? = How are you doing?
> → Sto bene, grazie. E Lei? = I'm doing well, thanks. And you?

There are also certain words that have a formal and informal counterpart:

- Salve (formal) = Hello / Goodbye
- Ciao (informal)

- Arrivederla (formal) = See you later
- Arrivederci (informal)

In this book, formal phrases will be noted with **(F)**

1

Verbs

Verbs are more complex in Italian than in English, because for every one of these action words, there are 6 different ways to say it, based on the subject pronouns seen on the previous page. It's important to say the correct conjugation in order to convey the subject you are intending. You'll see the rules for conjugating regular verbs in the following pages. Irregular verbs however, don't follow a pattern, and must be memorized.

In Italian, as already mentioned, there is a formal way of addressing people. It's used with people that you don't know well or wish to show respect. (e.g. your professor or doctor). Young Italians use the formal form with their elders, and adults use it with people they are less familiar with.

When you use the 3rd person singular, or the 'lui/lei/Lei' conjugation when speaking to someone, you are using the formal form. You can use the subject pronoun 'Lei' for emphasis. When you use 'tu' and its verb conjugation on the other hand, you are implying informality. When traveling, it's best to be extra polite, so use the 'lui/lei/Lei' conjugation when speaking to an Italian. He or she will appreciate the respectful approach. Although technically the 'loro' conjugation (and pronoun) should be used to convey the plural formal, it is acceptable to use the 'voi' form when speaking to a group. Contrast the following forms:

→ Lei, come sta? = How are you? (formal)
→ Tu, come stai? = How are you? (informal, singular)
→ Voi, come state? = How are you? (plural)

There is no 'do/does' when formulating a question. Turn a statement into a question simply by adding voice inflection.

→ Ballate. = You all dance.
→ Ballate? = Do you all dance?

2

Verbs - Present tense

In this book, only the present tense will be taught. You can use the present tense however, to express events that will happen in the near future.

There are two considerations of verbs in the present:

 : Have a specific formula that is applied to a specific group. Once the formula is memorized, it's easily plugged into any verb within that group. Will be designated by **(R)** in this book.

 : Don't follow a pattern and conjugations need to be memorized. Will be designated by **(I)**.

Regular verbs fall into one of the following three groups:

Ending in .. → **-are**

.. → **-ere**

.. → **-ire** (there are 2 types of -ire verbs, classified into either **set 1** or **2**).

When a verb ends in -are, -ere or -ire, it is in its infinitive form. This is the general meaning before it has been conjugated according to different subjects.

3

Regular verbs ending in -are

To communicate that an action is done by a certain person or people, you must change the verb from its infinitive or basic form to one agreeing with each subject pronoun. The subject pronouns are the foundation of a verb conjugation.

Step 1 → Remove the -are ending and place the root of the verb in each conjugation.

chiam~~are~~ = to call

(io)	chiam	(noi)	chiam
(tu)	chiam	(voi)	chiam
(lui/lei Lei)	chiam	(loro)	chiam

Step 2 → Add the formulaic ending specific to regular verbs ending in -are.

To make a sentence negative, put 'non' in front of the verb.
↓
Non chiamano = They don't call.

(io)	chiam**o**	(noi)	chiam**iamo**
(tu)	chiam**i**	(voi)	chiam**ate**
(lui/lei Lei)	chiam**a**	(loro)	chiam**ano**

4

-are verbs continued

Therefore, the formulaic ending for ALL regular verbs ending in -are is:

(io)	-o	(noi)	-iamo
(tu)	-i	(voi)	-ate
(lui/lei Lei)	-a	(loro)	-ano

Memorize this formula!

Note that the conjugation of lui (he), lei (she) and Lei (you-formal, singular) is the same. Here, it's more important to include the subject pronoun in order to clarify who the subject is, otherwise it's not necessary to put a subject pronoun before the conjugation. Subject pronouns are used mostly for emphasis, once a verb has been conjugated.

When a verb is conjugated in the present tense, each conjugation can have three different meanings:

(For example)

chiamo → I call.
→ I do call.
→ I am calling.

As mentioned earlier, the present tense can be used to express the near future. Therefore, 'Chiamo' can also mean 'I will call'.

-are verbs continued

If a regular verb ends in -iare, you do not double up the `i` in the `tu` and `noi` conjugations:

mangiare = to eat

(io)	mangio	*(noi)	mang**iamo**
* (tu)	mang**i**	(voi)	mangiate
(lui/lei Lei)	mangia	(loro)	mangiano

If a regular verb in -are ends in -care or -gare, you must add an `h` in the `tu` and `noi` conjugations before adding the formulaic ending:

cercare = to look for

(io)	cerco	*(noi)	cerc**hiamo**
* (tu)	cerc**hi**	(voi)	cercate
(lui/lei Lei)	cerca	(loro)	cercano

pagare = to pay for

(io)	pago	*(noi)	pag**hiamo**
* (tu)	pag**hi**	(voi)	pagate
(lui/lei Lei)	paga	(loro)	pagano

Regular verbs ending in -ere

The rules for conjugating verbs that end in -ere are the same as for the group ending in -are:

Step 1 → Remove the -ere ending and place the root in each conjugation.

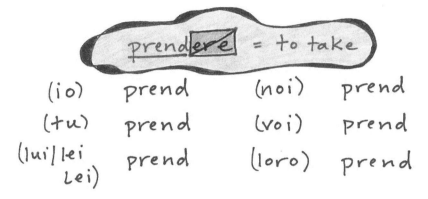

prend~~ere~~ = to take

(io)	prend	(noi)	prend
(tu)	prend	(voi)	prend
(lui/lei Lei)	prend	(loro)	prend

Step 2 → Add the formulaic ending specific to regular verbs ending in -ere.

(io)	prend**o**	(noi)	prend**iamo**
(tu)	prend**i**	(voi)	prend**ete**
(lui/lei Lei)	prend**e**	(loro)	prend**ono**

Therefore, the formulaic ending for ALL regular -ere verbs is:

(io)	-o	(noi)	-iamo
(tu)	-i	(voi)	-ete
(lui/lei Lei)	-e	(loro)	-ono

Memorize!

7

Regular verbs ending in -ire

As previously stated, there are two sets within this verb group:

Set 1 → Follow the same steps as when conjugating a regular verb ending in -are or -ere.
*Note how set 1 -ire verb conjugations are almost identical to those in the -ere group.

dormire = to sleep

(io)	dorm**o**	(noi)	dorm**iamo**
(tu)	dorm**i**	(voi)	dorm**ite**
(lui/lei Lei)	dorm**e**	(loro)	dorm**ono**

Therefore, the formulaic ending for ALL set 1 regular -ire verbs is:

(io)	-o	(noi)	-iamo
(tu)	-i	(voi)	-ite
(lui/lei Lei)	-e	(loro)	-ono

Memorize!

* Note that the conjugations of ALL regular verbs in -are, ere and set 1 -ire are identical in the 'io', 'tu' and 'noi' forms. The only difference between -ere verbs and set 1 -ire, is in the 'voi' form.

8

Regular verbs ending in -ire

Set 2 → The -ire verbs here are differentiated from those in set 1 by adding '-isc' before the formulaic endings of set 1 in all conjugations EXCEPT FOR `noi` and `voi`!

finire = to finish

(io)	fin**isco**	(noi)	fin**iamo**
(tu)	fin**isci**	(voi)	fin**ite**
(lui/lei Lei)	fin**isce**	(loro)	fin**iscono**

Therefore, the formulaic ending for set 2 -ire verbs is:

Yes, memorize this too!

io	-isco	noi	-iamo
tu	-isci	voi	-ite
lui/lei Lei	-isce	loro	-iscono

A way to identify if an -ire verb belongs in set 1 or 2 (most of the time), is to look at the infinitive form and count 5 letters back from the end. If the 5th letter back is a consonant, it belongs in set 1. If the 5th letter back is a vowel, it belongs in set 2. (Usually!)

dormire
5 . . . .
(set 1)

finire
5 . . . .
(set 2)

9

Reflexive Verbs

Reflexive verbs require a reflexive pronoun in front of the verb's conjugation to convey the action of the verb being reflected back to that person. Although their infinitive endings are -arsi, -ersi or -irsi, they are conjugated according to the rules for regular verbs ending in -are, -ere or -ire. (Unless they're irregular).

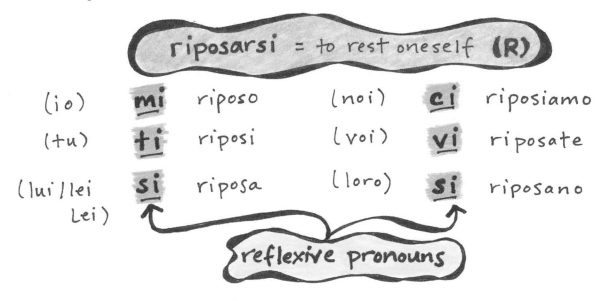

riposarsi = to rest oneself **(R)**

(io)	**mi** riposo	(noi)	**ci** riposiamo
(tu)	**ti** riposi	(voi)	**vi** riposate
(lui / lei / Lei)	**si** riposa	(loro)	**si** riposano

reflexive pronouns

Some common reflexive verbs:
- svegliarsi = to wake oneself **(R)**
- alzarsi = to get oneself up **(R)**
- chiamarsi = to call oneself **(R)**
- prepararsi = to prepare oneself **(R)**
- vestirsi = to get oneself dressed **(R)**
- mettersi = to put on clothing / to begin a task **(R)**
- fermarsi = to stop oneself **(R)**
- divertirsi = to enjoy oneself **(R)**
- sedersi = to sit down **(I)**

Reflexive Verbs continued

Irregular

sedersi = to sit down (I)

(io) mi siedo   (noi) ci sediamo
(tu) ti siedi   (voi) vi sedete
(lui/lei si siede   (loro) si siedono
   Lei)

- Non si siedono al concerto. = They're not sitting at the concert.

Certain verbs can be both reflexive and non-reflexive :

→ Mi chiamo Danielle. = My name is Danielle.
- Chiamo Danielle. = I'm calling Danielle.

→ Ci prepariamo. = We're getting ourselves ready.
- Prepariamo la cena. = We're preparing dinner.

Certain verbs can be used reciprocally in the plural forms :

- vedersi = to see each other
- incontrarsi = to meet each other   ← A few examples
- scriversi = to write each other
- conoscersi = to know each other

→ Ci vediamo domani. = We'll see each other tomorrow.
→ Vi incontrate in centro. = You'll meet each other downtown.

When making commands, attach the reflexive pronoun to the end of the command in the 'tu', 'noi' and 'voi' forms, but leave in front for the 'Lei' command.

→ Divertiti! = Have fun! ('Tu')
→ Alziamoci! = Let's get up! ('Noi')
→ Mettetevi una giacca! = Put a jacket on! ('Voi')
→ Si fermi! = Stop! ('Lei')

See commands, next pages.

Verbs - Commands

When you tell someone to do a certain action, the command or imperative forms for regular verbs are as follows:

	mangiare	prendere	dormire	finire
tu	mangia!	prendi!	dormi!	finisci!
Lei	mangi!	prenda!	dorma!	finisca!
voi	mangiate!	prendete!	dormite!	finite!
noi	mangiamo!	prendiamo!	dormiamo!	finiamo!

The 'tu' command is used when speaking to 1 person in an informal or familiar way. Note that the -are verb is the only verb group that doesn't use the present tense 'tu' conjugation for its informal 'tu' command.

The 'Lei' command is used when speaking to 1 person who you don't know well, or where the exchange is more formal.

The 'voi' command is used when addressing more than 1 person. It's fine to use it in informal or formal situations.

The 'noi' command translates to 'Let's __!'
'Mangiamo!' = Let's eat!

If you want to tell someone not to do something, simply put 'non' in front of the command. HOWEVER, ONLY IN THE 'tu' command, you will keep the verb in the infinitive form. 'Non dormire!' = Don't sleep! (You, singular, informal)

12

Irregular verb commands

The most frequently used commands of irregular verbs which also have some irregular imperative forms include the following verbs:

- avere = to have
- stare = to stay / be
- dare = to give
- fare = to do / make

- essere = to be
- andare = to go
- dire = to say / tell
- venire = to come

	avere	stare	dare	fare
tu	abbi!	sta'! or stai!	da'! or dai!	fa'! or fai!
Lei	abbia!	stia!	dia!	faccia!
voi	abbiate!	state!	date!	fate!
noi	abbiamo!	stiamo!	diamo!	facciamo!

	essere	andare	dire	venire
tu	sii!	va'! or vai!	di'!	vieni!
Lei	sia!	vada!	dica!	venga!
voi	siate!	andate!	dite!	venite!
noi	siamo!	andiamo!	diciamo!	veniamo!

13

Nouns

Every Italian noun has a number (singular or plural - just like English), and a gender (masculine or feminine - unlike English). Often, you can tell the gender and number of a noun by looking at the ending, and almost certainly when the definite article is included. There are exceptions, however!

Feminine nouns:

- If they end in **-a** in the singular, change to **-e** in the plural.
  → chies<u>a</u> (church) → chies<u>e</u> (churches)

- If they end in **-e** in the singular, change to **-i** in the plural.
  → stazion<u>e</u> (station) → stazion<u>i</u> (stations)

Masculine nouns:

- If they end in **-o** in the singular, change to **-i** in the plural.
  → teatr<u>o</u> (theater) → teatr<u>i</u> (theaters)

- If they end in **-e** in the singular, change to **-i** in the plural.
  → ristorant<u>e</u> (restaurant) → ristorant<u>i</u> (restaurants)

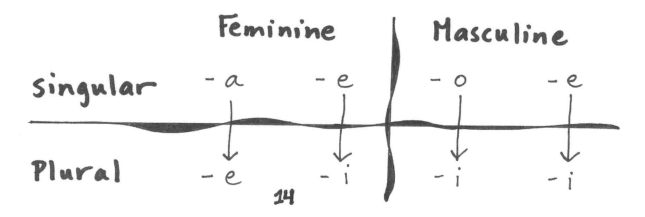

	Feminine		Masculine	
Singular	-a	-e	-o	-e
Plural	-e	-i	-i	-i

Nouns continued

- If a noun is abbreviated, it doesn't change forms in the plural.
  → una foto̲   → due foto̲
  (a picture)   (2 pictures)

- If a noun ends in (a consonant), it's considered masculine, and doesn't change forms when used in the plural.

  → un bar̲ (a coffee shop) → 2 bar̲ (2 coffee shops)

- If a noun ends in an (accented vowel) it also remains unmodified in the plural. Usually the à or ù means that it's feminine, and the è, ì or ò signifies a masculine noun.

  → una città̲ (a city) → 2 città̲ (2 cities)

 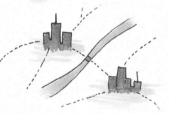

- If a noun ends in (-ca -go or -ga) (and sometimes -co), you must add an 'h̲' in the plural form.

  → un'amica (a friend (that's a girl)) → 2 amich̲e (2 friends that are girls)

  → un lago (a lake) → 2 lagh̲i (2 lakes)

15

Nouns continued — some important ones!

Days of the week: 'I giorni della settimana'

(il) lunedì = Monday
(il) martedì = Tuesday
(il) mercoledì = Wednesday
(il) giovedì = Thursday
(il) venerdì = Friday
(il) sabato = Saturday
(la) domenica = Sunday

Days, seasons, and months aren't capitalized in Italian. If you put the definite article in front of a day, it means 'every'!
→ **la domenica** = every Sunday

Seasons and months: 'Le stagioni e i mesi'

'In' or 'di' in front of the season means 'in the'.
→ **In estate** = In the summer
Use 'a' before months → **A marzo** = In March

(la) **primavera** (Spring)
• marzo = March
• aprile = April
• maggio = May

(l') **estate** (Summer)
• giugno = June
• luglio = July
• agosto = August

(l') **autunno** (Fall)
• settembre = September
• ottobre = October
• novembre = November

(l') **inverno** (Winter)
• dicembre = December
• gennaio = January
• febbraio = February

To say the date, use 'il' + 'number' + 'month'
↳ il 23 febbraio = February 23rd
For the first, use 'il primo' → **il primo gennaio** = January 1st

16

Adjectives

Adjectives describe nouns, and follow the same rules in terms of gender and number (See the chart on the following page). They either precede the noun (a small group), or follow the noun (most adjectives). Just as with nouns, those presented here ending in -o have 4 choices of endings based on gender and number. Those ending in -e only have 2 forms: singular and plural.

Usually precede the noun:

If they follow the noun, it's for emphasis

- bello = beautiful
- brutto = ugly
- bravo = talented
- giovane = young
- stesso = same
- primo = first
- poco = few

- piccolo = small
- grande = big
- nuovo = new
- vecchio = old
- ultimo = last
- molto = many
- troppo = too many / too much

- buono = good
- cattivo = bad, mean
- vero = true
- caro = dear
- altro = other
- tanto = many

* 'Molto', 'tanto', 'poco' and 'troppo' can also be used as adverbs in which case they don't change form.

This group ALWAYS precedes the noun.

* When 'caro' follows the noun, it means 'expensive'.

Follow the noun:

Add an 'h' in the feminine plural form.

- biondo = blond
- bruno = brunette
- grasso = fat
- interessante = interesting
- noioso = boring
- divertente = fun
- carino = cute

- simpatico = nice
- antipatico = unkind
- intelligente = smart
- energico = energetic
- stanco = tired
- tranquillo = calm
- comodo = comfortable

- alto = tall
- basso = short
- felice = happy
- contento = happy
- triste = sad
- gentile = kind
- scomodo = uncomfortable

Add an 'h' in the plural forms.

17

Adjectives continued

Colors:

- rosso = red
- verde = green
- giallo = yellow
- bianco = white
- nero = black
- grigio = gray
- azzurro = sky blue

Not capitalized in Italian.

These colors have invariable forms and don't ever change:

→ rosa = pink
→ viola = violet
→ blu = dark blue
→ arancione = orange
→ marrone = brown

Nationalities:

- americano = American
- italiano = Italian
- canadese = Canadian
- africano = African
- irlandese = Irish
- francese = French
- tedesco = German
- messicano = Mexican
- inglese = English
- spagnolo = Spanish

The same chart is used for figuring out the ending of both nouns and adjectives.

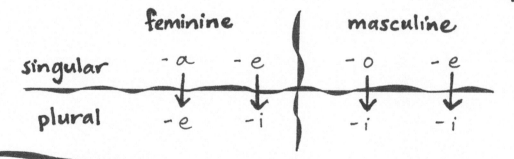

	feminine		masculine	
singular	-a ↓	-e ↓	-o ↓	-e ↓
plural	-e	-i	-i	-i

Examples:

Adjectives which precede the noun:

- Guido una piccola macchina. = I drive a small car.
- Molti studenti studiano italiano. = Many students study Italian.

18

Adjectives continued

Adjectives which follow the noun:

- Lui è un uomo gentile. = He is a nice man.
- Sono ragazzi canadesi. = They are Canadian kids.

You can also use the adjective separately from the noun:

→ La guida è tranquilla. = The guide is calm.
→ Siamo intelligenti. = We are smart.

Adverbs

Adverbs modify verbs, adjectives or another adverb - not NOUNS!
They usually say when, where, how, and how often something happens.

- bene = well   (Don't confuse with `buono', `bravo', `bello')
- male = poorly (Don't confuse with `cattivo')

→ Ballo bene. = I dance well.
→ Mangiano male. = They eat poorly.

As previously mentioned, `**molto**', `**tanto**', `**troppo**' and `**poco**'
are also adverbs. Their meaning changes slightly as adverbs,
and their form remains invariable.

→ Loro sono molto divertenti. = They are very fun.
→ Dormono tanto. = They sleep a lot.

Other important adverbs: Also an adjective with a different meaning

- ora = now
- presto = early
- tardi = late
- lentamente = slowly
- assolutamente = absolutely

- prima = before
- spesso = often
- già = already
- facilmente = easily
- probabilmente = probably

- sempre = always
- ancora = still
- mai = never
- rapidamente = quickly

19

Indefinite Articles

(a , an)

Masculine

* **un** – before all masculine nouns that begin with a vowel and most consonants

• **uno** – before all masculine nouns that begin with z, s + consonant, ps, gn

Feminine

* • **una** – before all feminine nouns that begin with a consonant

* most common

• **un'** – before all feminine nouns that begin with a vowel

• un passaporto = a passport
• uno zaino = a backpack
• un uomo = a man

• una borsa = a bag
• un'automobile = a car
• una donna = a woman

Most masculine singular nouns end in -o. Most feminine singular nouns end in -a. However, there are singular nouns that end in -e, which may be masculine or feminine. If a noun ends in a consonant, it is masculine.

Buono

Buono is an adjective and describes qualities of goodness regarding substance or character. It will usually precede the noun, although may be placed after the noun for emphasis. When 'buono' precedes the noun, it follows the same pattern as the indefinite article in the singular form:

Masculine :   un → **buon**   uno → **buono**

Feminine :   una → **buona**   un' → **buon'**

- un ristorante = a restaurant
  → un buon ristorante = a good restaurant

- uno studente = a male student
  → un buono studente = a good male student

- una bambina = a little girl
  → una buona bambina = a good little girl

- un' automobile = a car
  → una buon'automobile = a good car

> Note that the word directly preceding the noun is the only word that is modified. The indefinite article changes form when it is not directly preceding the noun.

In the plural form, there are only 2 forms of 'buono':

Masculine → **buoni**   ↗ i buoni ristoranti
                         ↘ i buoni studenti

Feminine → **buone**   ↗ le buone bambine
                         ↘ le buone automobili

Definite Articles = the

There are **8** different ways to say "The!" The article depends on whether the noun is singular/plural, masculine/feminine, and the letter with which it begins.

The article for both masculine and feminine singular nouns that begin with a vowel is the same = l'

	Masculine	**Feminine**
Singular	il - before most consonants l' - before all vowels lo - before z, s + consonant, ps or gn	la - before all consonants l' - before all vowels
Plural	i - the plural of `il'  gli - the plural of `l'' and `lo'	le - the plural of `la' & `l''

- il bar → i bar (If a noun ends in a consonant, it doesn't change in the plural).
- il museo → i musei
- l'albergo → gli alberghi (If a noun ends in -go, -ga, -ca, add an `h' in the plural).
- lo stadio → gli stadi ⟶ (If a noun ends in -io, don't double up the `i' unless the accent falls on the last `i'. eg → zio → zii)
- la stazione → le stazioni
- la chiesa → le chiese
- l'università → le università ⟶ (If a noun ends in an accent, it doesn't change in the plural).

22

Use of the Definite Article

In Italian, the definite article (the) is used more frequently than in English. It's required in the following situations:

- Before nouns, when used to express a concept or a category of things as a whole.

  → Mi piace la pizza. = I like pizza.

  → L'arte è importante. = Art is important.

- Before the names of languages, except when preceded by 'parlare' or 'studiare'.

  → L'italiano è bello. = Italian is beautiful.

  → Parlano spagnolo. = They speak Spanish.

- Before titles when talking about people, but not when talking to them.

  → Il professore Bianchi è simpatico = Prof. Bianchi is nice.

  → "Grazie, professore Bianchi" = Thank you, prof. Bianchi.

- Before days of the week, to indicate a habitual activity.

  → La domenica ceno con la mia famiglia = Every Sunday I eat dinner with my family.

- Before names of countries, states, regions, large islands, mountains & rivers.

  → Abito negli Stati Uniti. = I live in the United States.

  → La Sicilia è un'isola. = Sicily is an island.

Bello

'Bello' is an adjective that means beautiful or handsome, and describes a pleasing aesthetic quality or qualities. Like 'buono', 'bello' usually precedes the noun. When it follows the noun, it's intended for emphasis. While 'buono' is modified in accordance with the indefinite articles, 'bello' is changed to blend with the definite articles. Because there are 8 definite articles, there are 8 different forms of 'bello' when it directly precedes the noun.

Bello..

+ il = **Bel**	(il tiramisù) →	il <u>bel tiramisù</u>
+ lo = **Bello**	(lo zabaglione) →	il <u>bello zabaglione</u>
+ l' = **Bell'**	(l'antipasto) →	il <u>bell'antipasto</u>
+ i = **Bei**	(i ravioli) →	i <u>bei ravioli</u>
+ gli = **Begli**	(gli gnocchi) →	i <u>begli gnocchi</u>
+ la = **Bella**	(la pizza) →	la <u>bella pizza</u>
+ l' = **Bell'**	(l'insalata) →	la <u>bell'insalata</u>
+ le = **Belle**	(le lasagne) →	le <u>belle lasagne</u>

When 'bello' is used to describe food, it is referring to the way it looks, not the way it tastes. Use 'buono' to describe food that tastes good.

Note that when 'bello' is modified and directly precedes the noun, the definite article in front can change as well.

Prepositions

Prepositions can be difficult because the context will often determine their usage. They are explained more in depth within their respective letter of the alphabet.

a = to, at, in, by
→ often follows the verb 'andare'
→ used with..
- cities
- certain methods of transportation
- places

in = in, to, at, by on
→ can sometimes follow 'andare'
→ used with..
- regions and countries
- street names
- most methods of transportation
- places

di = of, from
→ also used to indicate possession

da = from
→ also used to indicate someone's house or business

su = on

con = with

per = for

fra / tra = between, among
→ often used with time

Articulated Prepositions

The prepositions `a`, `in`, `di`, `da` and `su` will often combine with the definite article to form these new words (articulated prepositions.)

+	masculine singular			masculine plural		feminine singular		feminine plural
	il	**lo**	**l'**	**i**	**gli**	**la**	**l'**	**le**
a	al	allo	all'	ai	agli	alla	all'	alle
in	nel	nello	nell'	nei	negli	nella	nell'	nelle
di	del	dello	dell'	dei	degli	della	dell'	delle
da	dal	dallo	dall'	dai	dagli	dalla	dall'	dalle
su	sul	sullo	sull'	sui	sugli	sulla	sull'	sulle

- Andiamo alla stazione. = We're going to the (train) station.
- Le chiavi sono nello zaino. = The keys are in the backpack.
- I libri sono degli studenti. = The books belong to the students.
- Partono dall'isola. = They're leaving from the island.
- C'è molta gente sulla spiaggia. = There are many people on the beach.

26

Possessive Pronouns

The possessive pronoun agrees in gender and number with the noun it describes, NOT the person who possesses it. Therefore, there are 4 ways to say each form. You will always include the definite article in front of the possessive pronoun, UNLESS you are talking about a family member in the singular OR if you place the noun in front of the pronoun. (e.g. casa mia). For space conservation on this page, the following words are abbreviated as follows:

masculine = M { feminine = F { singular = S { plural = P

mine	il mio (M,S) →	i miei (M,P)
	la mia (F,S) →	le mie (F,P)
yours (singular you)	il tuo (M,S) →	i tuoi (M,P)
	la tua (F,S) →	le tue (F,P)
his / hers / yours singular, formal	il suo (M,S) →	i suoi (M,P)
	la sua (F,S) →	le sue (F,P)
ours	il nostro (M,S) →	i nostri (M,P)
	la nostra (F,S) →	le nostre (F,P)
yours (plural you)	il vostro (M,S) →	i vostri (M,P)
	la vostra (F,S) →	le vostre (F,P)
their	il loro (M,S) →	i loro (M,P)
	la loro (F,S) →	le loro (F,P)

Direct Object Pronouns

The direct object of a sentence is the 'who' or 'what' referred to by the verb.

→ Mangio una pizza. = I'm eating pizza.

↑
direct object (what)

→ Porto Maria a casa. = I'm bringing Maria home.

↑
direct object (who)

If the sentence is negative, 'non' goes in front of the phrase → Non la mangio.

For easier communication (in order to not continue to repeat the direct object), you can replace the direct object with a pronoun. This pronoun is then moved directly in front of the verb. Here are the direct object pronouns:

mi = me

ti = you

la = her / you (formal)
= it (a feminine, singular object)

lo = him
= it (a masculine, singular object)

ci = us

vi = you (plural)

le = them (a group of girls)
= those (feminine, plural objects)

li = them (a group of guys, or guys and girls)
= those (masculine, plural objects)

singular feminine:

→ Mangio una pizza. → La mangio.
→ Porto Maria a casa. → La porto a casa.

28

Direct Object Pronouns continued

plural masculine:

li

→ Lavo i piatti. → Li lavo. (I'm washing the dishes.)

→ Vedo Fabio e Giorgio. → Li vedo. (I see Fabio and Giorgio.)

li

Some other examples:

• Incontro te. → Ti incontro. (I'm meeting you.)

ti   See section on disjunctive pronouns

• Invitano noi. → Ci invitano. (They're inviting us.)

ci

• Non saluta me mai. → Non mi saluta mai.
                         (He/she/ you never say hi.)

mi

You can attach the direct object pronoun to the end of commands in all forms except the singular formal (Lei).

→ Eccoci! = Here we are!

→ Prendilo! = Take it!

→ Mangiateli! = Eat them!

→ Finiamola! = Let's finish it!

29

Indirect Object Pronouns

The direct object is the 'what' or 'who' addressed by the verb, while the indirect object designates the person 'to whom' or 'for whom' the action is directed.

Look for the prepositions 'a' or 'per' followed by a disjunctive pronoun or someone's name, to help you find the indirect object.

indirect object (to whom)

• Scrivo una lettera a Gina. = I'm writing a letter to Gina.

direct object (what)

indirect object (for whom)

• Preparano una cena per noi. = They're preparing a dinner for us.

direct object (what)

Indirect and direct objects can also exist independently of each other :

→ Telefoni a tua madre. = You're calling your mom.

indirect object (to whom)

→ Chiami tua madre. = You're calling your mom.

direct object (who)

These 2 sentences mean the same thing, but 'telefonare' requires the use of 'a' afterwards, while 'chiamare' doesn't.

30

Indirect Object Pronouns continued

The following verbs will indicate the presence of an indirect object when their action is directed towards someone:

- chiedere = to ask for
- dare = to give
- offrire = to offer
- mandare = to send/mail
- portare = to bring/carry
- preparare = to prepare
- regalare = to give as a gift

- parlare = to speak
- dire = to say/tell
- domandare = to ask
- insegnare = to teach
- rispondere = to respond
- scrivere = to write
- telefonare = to call

As seen on the previous page, many of these verbs will be used with both an indirect and direct object:

indirect object (to whom)

- Insegna l'italiano agli studenti. = (She) teaches Italian to the (or He) students.

direct object (what)

indirect object (to whom)

- Offro un caffè a Marco. = I'm offering a coffee to Marco.

direct object (what)

2 verbs which always utilize an indirect object:
→ piacere = to be pleasing ⟶ See letter 'P' for more.
→ mancare = to lack

31

Indirect Object Pronouns continued

Just like direct objects, indirect objects have pronouns that can replace them. You'll notice a similarity between indirect object pronouns, direct object pronouns, and reflexive pronouns.

mi = to me
ti = to you
gli = to him
le = to her /
to you (formal)

ci = to us
vi = to you all
gli = to them
(masculine and feminine)

Always put the indirect object pronoun directly in front of the verb:

= le
• Telefono a Maria. → Le telefono.
(I'm calling Maria).

= vi
• Mandano un email a voi. → Vi mandano un email.
(They're sending an email to you all).

= gli
• A Fabio e Franco piace la pizza. → Gli piace la pizza.
(Pizza is pleasing to Fabio and Franco).

See letter 'P' for more on the verb 'piacere'.

Disjunctive Pronouns

These pronouns are used after a verb or preposition. Notice their similarity to subject pronouns.

me — me ; myself

te — you ; yourself (familiar)

lui — him

lei — her

Lei — you (formal)

sé — himself ; herself ; yourself

noi — us ; ourselves

voi — you ; yourselves (plural)

loro — them

sé — themselves

When saying that someone does something on their own, use the preposition `da`. If you're referring to `him`, `her`, `you formal` or `them`, use `sé`.

→ Marco impara l'italiano da sé.

(Marco is learning Italian on his own).

→ Loro cominciano da sé.

(They are starting on their own).

- Vedono me. = They see me.
- Questo è per te. = This is for you.
- Parlo a lui. = I'm talking to him.

`Da` followed by a disjunctive pronoun, also refers to someone's house or business.

→ Vado da lei. = I'm going to her (house).

33

A

sounds like 'ah'

- A = To | At | In | By

Use 'a' before cities and certain places like 'home':

→ A Roma = To | In Rome
→ A casa = To | At home

.. with these 2 ways to get around:

→ A piedi = By foot
→ A cavallo = By horse

.. with places in the city (the article will be articulated with 'a' → see page 26).

→ Al parco = To the | At the park
→ Alla farmacia = To the | At the pharmacy

See letter 'o' for more on telling time. →

- A che ora..? = At what time..?
  → A mezzogiorno. = At noon.
  → A mezzanotte. = At midnight.
  → All' una. = At 1:00.
  → Alle due, tre, quattro. = At 2:00, 3:00, 4:00.

- Arrivederla! = See you again! (F)
- Arrivederci! = See you again!
- A presto! = See you soon!
- A dopo! = See you later!
- A più tardi = See you later!

(*All of these are informal*)

- Addio = Farewell
- Accanto a = Next to
- Anche / Anch'io = Also / Me too
- Adesso = Now
- Ancora = Still
- Appunto = Exactly
- Assolutamente = Absolutely
- Aperto = Open

Allora

=

So, then, therefore

(A great word to use in conversation! Say when there's a lull or to change subjects. Use as a question to ask what's going on.)

→ Allora?

34

Nouns

A

(gli) • auguri = greetings, blessings

'Fare gli auguri' means to wish someone well. You can say 'Auguri' or 'Tanti auguri' or 'Auguroni' to convey best wishes on a special celebration or birthday. 'Tanti auguri a te' is the happy birthday song.

Don't include the definite article with months.

To say in a month, use 'a' or 'ad' if it starts with a vowel.
→ Ad aprile (In April)
Use 'in' or 'di' with seasons.
→ In autunno (In the Fall)

- aprile = April
- agosto = August
- (l') • autunno = Fall
- (l') • autobus = bus
- (l') • automobile = car
- (l') • aereo / aeroplano = airplane
- (l') • aeroporto = airport
- (l') • albergo = hotel (also use l'hotel)
- (l') • appartamento = apartment
- (l') • asciugamano = towel
- (l') • armadio = wardrobe
- (l') • antipasto = appetizer
  → anti = before
  → pasto = meal
- (l') • acqua = water
  → naturale = still water
  → frizzante / con gas = sparkling water
- (l') • aperitivo = late afternoon drink
  'L'ora dell'aperitivo' = Happy Hour!

- (l') • aglio = garlic
- (l') • arancia = orange (the fruit)
- (l') • amore = love
- (l') • appuntamento = date, appointment
- (l') • attenzione = attention
- (l') • aiuto = help
- (l') • aria = air
- (l') • anno = year
- (l') • allegria = cheerfulness
- (l') • albero = tree
- (l') • alba = dawn
- (l') • abbraccio = hug
- (l') • arte = art
- (l') • amico = friend (a guy)
- (l') • amica = friend (a girl)
- (gli) • amici = friends (girls and guys, or all guys)
- (le) • amiche = friends (all girls)

35

A

See letter 'V' for the rest of the conjugations

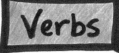 **Verbs**

* Both of these verbs are irregular and only have 2 conjugations that begin with 'A'

1) andare = to go (I)

(noi) andiamo = We go, We're going
(voi) andate = You all go, You're all going

Remember, you don't need to include 'noi' and 'voi' in front of the conjugation. Subject pronouns are used mainly for emphasis.

• Andiamo a Venezia. = We're going to Venice.
• Andate a mangiare. = You all are going to eat.

To say you're going to go do another action follow this formula:
conjugate andare + a + infinitive verb

2) avere = to have (I) → See letter 'H' for the rest of the conjugations.

(noi) abbiamo = We have, We're having
(voi) avete = You all have, You're all having

• Abbiamo una prenotazione. = We have a reservation.
• Avete tre automobili. = You all have three cars.

Use 'avere' in a literal sense, or with the following nouns to form idiomatic expressions:

- fame = hunger
- sete = thirst
- freddo = cold
- caldo = hot
- fretta = haste
- ragione = reason
- paura = fear
- voglia di _ = desire for _
- bisogno di _ = need of _
- _ anni = age

Follow with a noun or infinitive verb.

• Abbiamo fame. = We are hungry.
• Avete caldo. = You all are hot.
• Abbiamo voglia di un gelato. = We want an ice cream.

Verbs

* Review the verb section in the beginning of the book in case you forgot how to conjugate regular verbs.

3) **arrivare** = to arrive (R)

(io) **arrivo** = I'm arriving
I arrive
I do arrive

(tu) **arrivi** = You're arriving
You arrive
You do arrive

(lui | lei **arriva** = He | she | You formal..
Lei) is | are arriving
arrives | arrive
does | do arrive

(noi) **arriviamo** = We're arriving
We arrive
We do arrive

(voi) **arrivate** = You all are arriving
You all arrive
You all do arrive

(loro) **arrivano** = They're arriving
They arrive
They do arrive

From this point on, all 3 translations for each conjugation will not be written for conservation of space. And remember that the present tense can also be used to express the near future.

• Arrivo a mezzogiorno. = I arrive at noon.

• A che ora arriva il treno? = At what time does the train arrive?

A  Verbs

In the 'io', 'tu' and 'lui/lei/Lei' forms, the accent will fall on the first syllable.

4) abitare = to live (R)

(io) àbito = I live

(tu) àbiti = You live

(lui/lei àbita = He/she lives
  Lei) = You formal live

(noi) abitiamo = We live

(voi) abitate = You all live

(loro) abitano = They live

- E Lei, dove abita? = And you (formal), where do you live?
- Abitano a San Francisco. = They live in San Francisco.

5) aspettare = to wait for (R)

The preposition 'for' is included in the verb's meaning.

(io) aspetto = I wait for

(tu) aspetti = You wait for

(lui/lei aspetta = He/she waits for
  Lei) = You formal wait for

(noi) aspettiamo = We wait for

(voi) aspettate = You all wait for

(loro) aspettano = They wait for

- Aspettate l'autobus. = You all are waiting for the bus.
- Aspetto il treno. = I'm waiting for the train.

6) affittare = to rent (a house/apartment) (R)

Conjugate on your own!

(io) _____

(tu) _____

(lui/lei _____
  Lei)

(noi) _____

(voi) _____

(loro) _____

38

B

- Buona sera = Hello / Goodbye (in the evening) **(F)**
- Buona giornata! = Have a good day!
- Buona serata! = Have a good evening!
- Buon appetito! = Enjoy your food!
- Buon viaggio! = Have a good trip!
- Buon Natale! = Merry Christmas
- Buona Pasqua! = Happy Easter!
- Basta così = That's enough → *Use when purchasing food at the market to say the amount is good.*
- Benvenuti = Welcome (all of you)
- Bene = Well (an adverb - describes a verb, not a noun, so the end stays the same)
- Benissimo = Really well. (Also can be used as a positive exclamation on its own

Italians like to wish each other well on events throughout the day, by placing a form of **'Buono'** *in front of the noun.*
→ **Buono studio!** = *Enjoy studying!*

Buon giorno (F)
=
Hello / Goodbye
(during the day)

An extremely important phrase to remember! Use with people you have just met or aren't well acquainted with.

You can add -issimo to adjectives and adverbs to make the word more exaggerated.

- Bella = Beautiful (feminine, singular)
  → Bellissima! = Really beautiful!
- Buoni = Good (masculine, plural)
  → Buonissimi! = Really good!
- Brave = Capable (feminine, plural)
  → Bravissime! = Really capable!

Note how the gender and number of the adjectives 'bella,' 'buoni' and 'brave' above retain the same ending when -issimo is added. 'Benissimo' however, remains unmodified.

Nouns

B

(il) • bacio = Kiss

Italians usually great each other with two or even three light Kisses on the cheek.

(la) • bicicletta = bicycle
(`la bici' = biKe)

(la) • banca = bank

(il) • bar = coffee shop
(also called `il caffè)

(il) • binario = train platform

(il) • bagno = bathroom / bath
(`fare un bagno' = to take a bath / swim)

(la) • bambola = doll

(il) • bambino = little boy

(la) • bambina = little girl

(i) • bambini = little boys or boys and girls

(le) • bambine = little girls

(il) • biglietto = ticket, card
(for the train, bus, subway)

(il) • bicchiere = glass
(to drink from)

(la) • bottiglia = bottle

(la) • birra = beer

(la) • bibita / bevanda = drink

(il) • biscotto = cookie

(il) • basilico = basil

(la) • basilica = a church given special privileges by the Pope

(la) • brioche = pastry
(pronounced `bree-ósh')

Italians eat smaller breakfasts, usually consisting of a `brioche' or `pasta' and coffee, tea or juice.

(il) • berretto = (baseball) cap

Purchase your ticket for the `autobus' beforehand at the `Tabacchi' or `Tabaccaio'. Subway and train tickets can be purchased at the station. You can get train tickets online as well.

B

1) bere = to drink (I)

(io) bevo = I drink

(tu) bevi = You drink

(lui/lei Lei) beve = He/she drinks
= You formal drink

(noi) beviamo = We drink

(voi) bevete = You all drink

(loro) bevono = They drink

- Bevo una birra al bar. = I'm drinking a beer at the caffè.
- Bevono l'acqua naturale. = They're drinking still water.

2) ballare = to dance (R)

(io) ballo = I dance

(tu) balli = You dance

(lui/lei Lei) balla = He/she dances
= You formal dance

(noi) balliamo = We dance

(voi) ballate = You all dance

(loro) ballano = They dance

- Balli in cucina. = You dance in the kitchen.
- Balli in cucina? = Do you dance in the kitchen?

You can take any statement and make it a question simply by adding inflection.

41

C

Sounds like 'ch' in 'church' before **e** or **i**

cena → (chay·nah)

Sounds like 'K' in 'Key' before **a**, **o**, **u**, **h**

chi → (Kee)

- Ciao = Hi / Bye (informal) Use if Italians say first. Otherwise, say 'Salve', 'Buon giorno', 'Buona sera'
- Come sta? = How are you doing? **(F)**
- Come va? = How's it going?

Answers to both questions

→ Bene = Well
→ Benissimo = Really well
→ Non c'è male = Not bad
→ Tutto a posto = Everything's in place
→ Così così = OK
→ Male = Badly

- Come si chiama? = What's your name? **(F)**
  → Mi chiamo __. = My name is __.
- Chi = Who
- Cosa / Che / Che cosa = What (All 3 are interchangeable)
- Che c'è? = What's wrong? (pronounced 'Kay chay'?)
- Cosa vuol dire? = What does it mean?
  * Ask to define a word in English.
  → Cosa vuol dire ciao? (What does 'ciao' mean?)
- Come si dice? = How do you say?
  * Ask to define a word in Italian.
  → Come si dice 'hi'? (How do you say hi?)
- Ci credo = I believe it (Non ci credo = I don't believe it)

Che bello !
=
How beautiful !

(Use as a positive affirmation/exclamation in many situations).

* Use 'che' before an adjective to mean 'how'
→ **Che grande!** = How big!

Use 'che' before a noun to mean 'what'
→ **Che gioia!** = What joy!

42

C

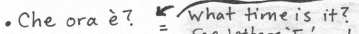

Words + Phrases

- Che ora è? ←= ⟍ *What time is it?*
- Che ore sono? ←   *See letters 'E' and 'S' for responses.*
- C'è = There is
- Ci sono = There are

You can change 'c'è' and 'ci sono' into questions simply by adding inflection at the end.

→ C'è un bagno. = There is a bathroom.
   C'è un bagno? = Is there a bathroom?

→ Ci sono le cartoline. = There are postcards.
   Ci sono le cartoline? = Are there postcards?

See letter 'F','T' for more ways to describe weather →

- Che tempo fa? = What's the weather like?
- → C'è il sole. = There's sun.
- → C'è il vento. = There's wind.
- → C'è la pioggia. = There's rain.
- → C'è la neve. = There's snow.
- → Ci sono le nuvole. = There are clouds.
- con = with
- Certo / Certamente = Certainly
- Comunque = Anyway
- Cioè = That is
- Così = This, like this
- Chiuso = Closed
- Complimenti! / Congratulazioni! = Compliments, congratulations
- Cin cin! = Cheers!

Use 'ci' also to replace a noun regarding location:
- Vai al mercato? (Are you going to the market?)
→ **Sì, ci vado.** (Yes, I'm going there.)

Così così = so so and answers the questions → Come sta? or → Come va?

The sound the glass makes when it clinks.. Also say, 'Salute!'

43

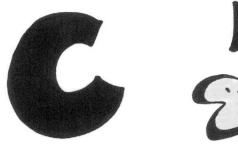

Nouns

'Il caffè'

'**Il caffè**' can refer to a drink or location - both of which are important aspects of Italian life! When referring to a location, it's a coffee shop, and can be used interchangeably with the word 'bar'. At the 'bar' or 'caffè', one can eat breakfast which includes a wide variety of coffee drinks (Italians invented espresso culture after all), teas, juices and pastries. Lunch is also served at the 'caffè', including various types of sandwiches, and drinks such as beer, wine, soda and water. You can sometimes even find 'gelato' or ice cream at the caffè. Because coffee is consumed all day in Italy, you can stop in anytime and even quickly, for a fast pick-me-up. You will pay more if you sit at a table than stand at the bar..!

Some common Italian coffee drinks:
- caffè = espresso (consumed any time of day, and frequently after meals)
- caffè latte = espresso with substantial milk (usually only consumed at breakfast)
- cappuccino = espresso with some milk and foam (usually only consumed up until lunch)
- caffè macchiato = espresso with a couple drops of hot milk
- caffè corretto = espresso with a shot of liquer
- caffè americano = espresso with some hot water
- caffè d'orzo = barley coffee with no caffeine

44

C

Nouns

(il) • centro = downtown

(la) • chiesa = church

(la) • cattedrale = cathedral (Duomo)

(il) • cinema = movie theater

(la) • casa = house

(la) • camera = room

(la) • cucina = kitchen

(il) • corridoio = hall /corridor

(la) • chiave = key

(la) • coperta = blanket /cover

(il) • cestino = wastebasket

(il) • cuscino = pillow

(il) • cibo = food   (la)

(il) • cameriere /cameriera = (waiter / waitress)

(il) • conto = bill

(la) • cena = dinner

(la) • carne = meat

(la) • cipolla = onion

(la) • carota = carrot

(il) • contorno = vegetable food course (sometimes called 'verdure')

(la) • coppa = cup (for gelato ⇒ ice cream)

(la) • città = city

(la) • campagna = countryside

• collina = hill (la)

(il) • canale = canal (like in Venice)

(il) • confine = border

(la) • cartolina = postcard

(il) • calcio = soccer (both popular

(il) • ciclismo = Italian sports !.)

(il) • concerto = concert

(il) • corpo = body   ↓

(il) • cuore = heart   cycling

(i) • capelli = hair(s)

(il) • cappello = hat

(la) • collana = necklace

> Ask for the bill when you want to leave the restaurant: ' Il conto, per favore!'

(i) • carabinieri = military police

> In Italy you will see military policemen and also 'la polizia', a civilian police force.

45

C

'chiamarsi' means 'to call oneself', used reflexively.

1) chiamare = to call (R)

(io) chiamo = I call

(tu) chiami = You call

(lui/lei chiama = He/she calls
  Lei) = You formal call

(noi) chiamiamo = We call

(voi) chiamate = You all call

(loro) chiamano = They call

- Chiamiamo il ristorante. = We're calling the restaurant.
- Chiamo Marco domani. = I'll call Marco tomorrow.

Remember that the present tense can also be used to express the near future.

Remember to add the 'h' in the 'tu' and 'noi' forms

2) cercare = to look for (R)

(io) cerco = I look for

(tu) cerchi = You look for

(lui/lei cerca = He/she looks for
  Lei = You formal look for

(noi) cerchiamo = We look for

(voi) cercate = You all look for

(loro) cercano = They look for

- Cerchi la chiave. = You're looking for the key.
- Cercano il museo. = They're looking for the museum.

C

Verbs

Often, Italians will ask if you understood what they said in the past tense.

Ha capito? (F) = Did you understand?

→ Si, ho capito. = Yes, I understood.

→ No, non ho capito. = No, I didn't understand.

3) capire = to understand **(R)** (set 2)

(io) capisco = I understand

(tu) capisci = You understand

(lui/lei capisce = He/she understands
Lei) = You formal understand

(noi) capiamo = We understand

(voi) capite = You all understand

(loro) capiscono = They understand

When you want to make a sentence negative, simply put '**non**' directly in front of the verb conjugation.

- Non capisci l'inglese. = You don't understand English.
- Non capiscono la professoressa. = They don't understand the (female) professor.

4) conoscere = to meet for the first time, to Know (a person or place) **(R)**

(io) conosco = I know

(tu) conosci = You Know

(lui/lei conosce = He/she Knows
Lei) = You formal Know

(noi) conosciamo = We Know

(voi) conoscete = You all Know

(loro) conoscono = They Know

- Piacere di conoscerla! = Pleasure to meet you (formal)! **(F)**
- Conosco un buon ristorante. = I Know a good restaurant.
- Lei conosce Fabio. = She Knows Fabio. / You know Fabio.

The verb 'sapere' also means 'to Know', but referring to a fact.

Conjugate these regular verbs on your own!

5) comprare = to buy (R)

(io) _____

(tu) _____

(lui/lei Lei) _____

(noi) _____

(voi) _____

(loro) _____

6) cominciare = to begin (R)

(io) _____

(tu) _____

(lui/lei Lei) _____

(noi) _____

(voi) _____

(loro) _____

7) cenare = to have dinner (R)

(io) _____

(tu) _____

(lui/lei Lei) _____

(noi) _____

(voi) _____

(loro) _____

D

Accent is on the first syllable, contrasted with `Dov'è`

- Dove = Where
- Dove sono..? = Where are..? (Used with plural nouns)
  → Dove sono i francobolli? (Where are the stamps?)
- Dentro = Inside
- Da = From, at/to someone's house or business
  → Da Viareggio = From Viareggio
  → Da Alessandro = At/to Alessandro's house
- Da dove viene? **(F)** = Where do you come from?
  → Vengo da Roma. (I'm from Rome.)

'Da' and 'di' both can mean from. 'Di' is usually just used with the verb 'essere' to mean "from" and 'da' is used with all other verbs.

- Di = Of, from, belonging to
  → Di Gina = Belonging to Gina
  → Il corso di biologia = The biology course
  → Di Salerno = From Salerno
- Di dov'è Lei? **(F)** = Where are you from?
  → Sono di Padova. (I'm from Padua.)
- Di solito = Usually
- Di nuovo = Again
- Di niente = You're welcome, no problem
- Di mattina = In the morning
- Del pomeriggio = In the afternoon
- Di sera = In the evening
- Di notte = At night

Times of day

- Dai! = Come on!
- Domani = Tomorrow
- Dimmi! = Tell me!
- Mi dica! **(F)** = Tell me!

Dov'è..?
=
Where is..?

(An important question for traveling! Follow with a singular noun.)
→ **Dov'è il mercato?**
=
where is the market?

- Dammi! = Give me!
- Destra = Right
  (A destra = To the right)

D

Words + Phrases

More food places are found under the letter 'M'.

As seen on the previous page, use **Dov'è .. ?** (Where is .. ?) with places in the city:

- la chiesa = church
- il Duomo = main cathedral
- il cinema = movie theater
- il teatro = live theater
- la libreria = bookstore
- il parco = park
- la stazione = (train) station
- lo stadio = stadium

- il supermercato = supermarket
- il mercato = outdoor market
- il fruttivendolo = produce shop
- il tabaccaio = odds and ends shop
- la pasticceria = pastry shop
- il panificio = bread shop
- la farmacia = pharmacy
- il negozio = store

Many words involving directions begin with 'D':

- dov'è ? = where is?
- dietro = behind
- dopo = after / afterwards
- davanti (a) = in front (of)
- dritto = straight

→ Scusi, **dov'è** il Duomo? = Excuse me, where is the cathedral?

- Vada sempre **dritto** in Via Dante. = Go straight on Dante Street.
- Poi, giri a **destra dopo** il parco. = Then, turn right after the park.
- Il Duomo è **dietro** la libreria e **davanti** alla farmacia.

= The Duomo is behind the bookstore and in front of the pharmacy.

50

Nouns

(la) • domenica = Sunday
• dicembre = December

(la) • domanda = question

(il) • diritto = (one's) right
(also means 'straight ahead')

(la) • destra = right (the direction)

(il) • dolce = dessert
(also the adjective, 'sweet')

(il) • digestivo = hard alcohol consumed after a meal to aid in digestion

(la) • direzione = direction

see commands pages 12, 13 for review

When asking directions, remember these phrases:

→ **Giri** or **Gira** or **Girate**
(Turn)

→ **a destra** (to the right)
→ **a sinistra** (to the left)

→ **Vada** or **Vai** or **Andate sempre dritto / diritto**
(Go)
(straight ahead)

see articulated prepositions, page 26

'Di' combined with the definite article can also mean 'some'.
• del pane = some bread • dei biscotti = some cookies
• delle domande = some questions

Verbs

1) **dovere** = to have to / must (I)

(io) devo   (noi) dobbiamo
(tu) devi   (voi) dovete
(lui/lei deve   (loro) devono
Lei)

From now on, the definitions of each conjugation won't be written. Refer to the grammar section if you need help!

• Lei deve partire domani. = She / You (formal) must leave tomorrow.
• Dobbiamo studiare. = We have to study.

'Dovere' is called a modal verb. It's usually conjugated, then followed by another verb in its infinitive form. See also 'potere' and 'volere'.

51

D

2) **dire** = to say/tell (**I**)

(io) dico   (noi) diciamo
(tu) dici   (voi) dite
(lui/lei dice   (loro) dicono
   Lei)

- Dite la verità. = You all tell the truth.
- Come si dice.? = How do you say.?

Use when you want to find out how to say a word in Italian.

3) **dare** = to give (**I**)

(io) do   (noi) diamo
(tu) dai   (voi) date
(lui/lei dà   (loro) danno
   Lei)

The word 'dai' is used commonly to mean, 'come on.'

- Do il libro a lei. = I'm giving the book to her.
- Dammi la penna! = Give me the pen! (Command form)
                                                          - tu

3) **desiderare** = to desire/want (**R**)

(io) desidero   (noi) desideriamo
(tu) desideri   (voi) desiderate
(lui/lei desidera   (loro) desiderano
   Lei)

Use 'avere voglia' and 'volere' to express desire as well.

- Desideri un caffè? = Do you want a coffee?
- Desiderano viaggiare in Italia. = They want to travel to Italy.

'Desiderare' like 'dovere', if followed by another action, will be conjugated and followed with an infinitive verb.

52

E

Pronounced with an open 'ay' sound, or a closed 'eh'

- Eccomi! = Here I am!
- Eccolo! = Here it is! / Here he is!
- Eccola! = Here it is! / Here she is!

See the direct object pronouns in the grammar sections, for more choices.

- Esatto / Esattamente = Exactly, correct
- E = And

The word for is = è, pronounced the same but written with an accent. See verbs, next page.

Ecco!

=

Here!

(Used when giving something to someone. Often has a direct object pronoun attached).

Nouns

(l') • estate = Summer

(l') • entrata = entrance

(l') • espresso = shot of coffee, interchangeable with 'caffè'. (Also, an express train).

(l') • est = east

E

Only 1 conjugation begins with 'e'. See letter 's' for the rest.

essere = to be (I)

(lui/lei) **è** = He/she/it is

(Lei) **è** = You (formal) are

Use 'essere' to describe being in a location :

→ Lui è a casa. = He is at home.

→ Lei è in Italia. = She is in Italy.

→ Scusi Lei, è a Torino? = Excuse me, are you (formal) in Torino?

Use 'essere' with adjectives : ← See grammar section for refresher on adjectives.

→ La casa è bella. = The house is beautiful.

→ Lui è felice. = He's happy.

→ Signora, Lei è molto gentile. = Ma'am, you're very kind.

Use 'essere' with telling time. The following times are the only ones that are expressed in the singular form, using è. Otherwise, use 'sono' - see letter 'O' (Ora).

→ È mezzogiorno. = It's noon.

→ È mezzanotte. = It's midnight.

→ È l'una. = It's 1.00.

F

We will begin the letter 'F' with the verb section, because so many important expressions utilize the verb 'fare'.

1) fare = to do/make (I)

(io) faccio	(noi) facciamo
(tu) fai	(voi) fate
(lui/lei / Lei) fa	(loro) fanno

'Fare' can be used literally:

→ Faccio una pizza. = I'm making a pizza.

→ Fanno i compiti. = They're doing homework.

'Fare' can also be used in the following idiomatic expressions:

fare colazione = to have breakfast
.. la spesa = to go grocery shopping
.. le spese = to shop for things other than food
.. una foto = to take a picture
.. una passeggiata = to take a walk
.. un bagno = to take a bath/swim
.. una doccia = to take a shower
.. un viaggio = to take a (big) trip
.. una pausa = to take a break
.. un pisolino = to take a nap
.. una festa = to throw a party
.. una domanda = to ask a question
.. ginnastica = to exercise, work out

55

F

Use 'fare' to describe the weather. See letters 'C' and 'T' for more expressions.

Che tempo fa? = what's the weather doing?
(How's the weather?)

→ Fa bel tempo | Fa bello. = It's nice out.

→ Fa brutto tempo | Fa brutto. = It's not nice out.

→ Fa caldo. = It's hot.

→ Fa freddo. = It's cold.

→ Fa fresco. = It's cool.

Use 'fare' to express a bodily ache / pain.

Mi + (fa or fanno) + male + body part

a singular body part

plural body parts

- la testa = head
- la gola = throat
- la schiena = back
- l'occhio = eye → gli occhi = eyes
- l'orecchio = ear → le orecchie = ears
- il dente = tooth → i denti = teeth
- il braccio = arm → le braccia = arms
- la mano = hand → le mani = hands
- la gamba = leg → le gambe = legs
- il piede = foot → i piedi = feet
- il ginocchio = knee → le ginocchia = knees

- la pancia / lo stomaco = stomach
- il naso = nose
- la bocca = mouth

Many body parts have irregular forms in the singular, plural, or both.

56

Mi fa male..

→ It hurts..

You can also use the verb 'avere' to say you have a bodily pain.
→ Ho mal di gola.
= I have a sore throat.

To say 'I'm sick', use the verb 'essere' + 'ammalato' (an adjective).
Sono ammalata.
= I'm sick.
(referring to a girl).

Mi fa male lo stomaco/la pancia.
(My stomach hurts.)

Mi fanno male i piedi.
(My feet hurt.)

Mi fa male la testa.
(My head hurts.)

Remember to make the form of 'fare' agree with the noun in regards to being singular (fa), or plural (fanno).

F

(2nd set -ire)

↓

2) finire = to finish (R)

(io)	finisco	(noi)	finiamo
(tu)	finisci	(voi)	finite
(lui/lei Lei)	finisce	(loro)	finiscono

The question, 'Did you finish?' is :
`Ha finito?' (F)
→ Si, ho finito.
=
Yes, I finished.
→ No, non ho finito.
=
No, I didn't finish.

• Lui finisce la lettera. = He's finishing the letter.
• Finite la cena. = You all are finishing dinner.

3) frequentare = to attend an event/class (R)

(io)	frequento	(noi)	frequentiamo
(tu)	frequenti	(voi)	frequentate
(lui/lei Lei)	frequenta	(loro)	frequentano

• Frequenti una partita di calcio. = You're attending a soccer game.
• Frequentiamo la lezione. = We're attending class.

Words + Phrases

Figurati
=
Don't mention it, of course.

(A way to say, no problem, you're welcome)

An important element of Italian culture, underlying behavior.

• Fra = Between/Among can be used with time to mean around
• Fra poco = Soon
• Fa = Ago (Use with periods of time. 'Un'ora fa' = An hour ago)   See page 99
• (Le) faccio sapere = I'll let you Know (F)
• (Le) faccio vedere = I'll show you (F)
• Fammi sapere = Let me know ⎫ (informal)
• Fammi vedere = Show me ⎭
• **Fare la bella figura** = To make a good impression
• Fuori = Outside

58

F

(la) • frutta = fruit

(la) • mela = apple
(la) • banana = banana
(l') • uva = grapes
(la) • pera = pear
(la) • fragola = strawberry
(l') • albicocca = apricot
(l') • arancia = orange
(il) • melone = melon
(l') • ananas = pineapple

(il) • pompelmo = grapefruit
(la) • pesca = peach
(il) • limone = lemon
(l') • anguria = watermelon
(il) • fico = fig
(la) • susina = plum
(il) • mirtillo = blueberry
(il) • mandarino = mandarin orange

(il) • freddo = cold
(la) • fame = hunger
(la) • fretta = haste
(la) • fortuna = luck
(il) • fastidio = annoyance
(la) • fantasia = imagination
(la) • fede = faith
(la) • febbre = fever
(la) • firma = signature
(la) • festa = party / holiday
(la) • ferrovia = railway
(il) • fine settimana = weekend
(la) • fine = end

• febbraio = February
(la) • farmacia = pharmacy
(il) • fruttivendolo = produce shop
(la) • farina = flour
(il) • fiore = flower
(il) • formaggio = cheese
(la) • farfalla = butterfly
(il) • fiume = river
(la) • fotografia = photograph
(abbreviated to 'la foto')
(la) • finestra = window
(il) • francobollo = stamp

59

F

Nouns - 'Feste'

Festa → Literally, a party that you attend or give. Also, a religious or civil holiday. Italy is predominantly Catholic, so many holidays are associated with the Church. Also called `i giorni festivi'.

> On International Women's Day, women are given mimosa flowers.

Ferie → Describes a vacation or holiday that people take, usually, but not always in the month of August.

Ferragosto → Coincides with the Catholic Feast of the Assumption of Mary. August was made the most popular vacation month by Roman Emperor Augustus. Celebrated August 15th.

The most popular Italian holidays other than Easter (Pasqua) and Christmas (Natale):

- The Epiphany (Epifania/La Befana) → Commemorates the 3 wise men's visit to Jesus. Celebrated January 6th

- Carnival (Carnevale) → The last celebration before Lent begins on Ash Wednesday.

- Republic Day (La Festa della Repubblica) → A celebration of the birth of the Italian Republic, a former monarchy. Observed June 2nd

- The Immaculate Conception (La Festa dell' Immacolata) → Celebrated December 8th to honor the Virgin Mary.

60

G

The pronunciation of the letter 'g' follows these rules:

1) When 'g' is followed by 'e' or 'i' it sounds like the 'j' in 'jelly'.
   → giacca = jacket (jah·kah)
   → gelato = ice cream (jeh·lah·to)

2) When 'g' is followed by 'a', 'o', 'u' or 'h', it sounds like the 'g' in 'gum'.
   → ghiaccio = ice (gee·ah·cho)
   → guida = guide (gwee·dah)

3) When 'g' is followed by 'n', it sounds like the 'ny' in 'canyon'.
   → gnocchi = potato dumplings (nyoh·kee)
   → montagna = mountain (mohn·tah·nyah)

4) When 'g' is followed by 'l', there are 2 possibilities of sounds:

   ⓐ enunciated :
      → gloria = glory (gloh·ree·ah)
      → gladiolo = gladiolus (glah·dee·oh·lo)

   ⓑ blended :
      → figlio = son (fee·lee·oh)
      → glielo = it to him (lee·eh·lo)

The blended sound of the 'gl' comes from the back of your throat. Contrast this with the sharp 'l' sound in ⓐ that comes from putting the tip of your tongue on the roof of your mouth.

G

Nouns

- gennaio = January
- giugno = June
- (il) giovedì = Thursday
- (il) gabinetto = lavatory, toilet
- (la) gente = people
- (la) grazia = grace
- (il) guardaroba = wardrobe, cloakroom
- (la) guardia = guard
- (il) giorno = day →
- (la) giornata = day
- (il) giornale = newspaper
- (il) gelato = ice cream
- (la) gelateria = ice cream shop
- (la) grappa = hard alcohol consumed after a meal
- (il) ghiaccio = ice
- (gli) gnocchi = potato dumplings
- (il) gusto = taste
- (la) guida = guide (a person or manual)
- (la) gonna = skirt
- (il) gatto = cat
- (la) gita = a day trip
- (il) girasole = sunflower
- (il) giardino = garden, yard →

`giornata` usually refers to what takes place in the day from morning to night

Use the word `orto` for vegetable garden

Grazie!
=
Thank you!

(You can modify in the following ways):

→ Grazie mille!
→ Mille grazie!
→ Molte grazie!
→ Tante grazie!

All of these mean `thanks a lot' or `many thanks'

See letter `M' for more ways to modify `grazie'

Words + Phrases

- Giri a destra! (F) = Turn right!
- Già = Already
- Giù = Down, below
- Giusto = Correct
- Gratis = Free
- Giorno festivo = Holiday

G

1) guardare = to watch / look at (R)

(io) guardo   (noi) guardiamo
(tu) guardi   (voi) guardate
(lui/lei guarda   (loro) guardano
    Lei)

Direct object pronoun - see grammar section

- Guardiamo un film! = Let's watch a movie!
- Mi guardano. = They're looking at me.

'Suonare' is the verb used with playing an instrument.

2) giocare = to play a game / sport (R)

(io) gioco   (noi) giochiamo
(tu) giochi   (voi) giocate
(lui/lei gioca   (loro) giocano
    Lei)

Remember to add an 'h' in the 'tu' and 'noi' conjugations

Add 'a' after 'giocare'

- Giochi a tennis. = You play tennis.
- Giocate spesso a calcio? = Do you all often play soccer?

3) girare = to turn (R)

(io) giro   (noi) giriamo
(tu) giri   (voi) girate
(lui/lei gira   (loro) girano
    Lei)

Use these command forms when giving directions.

- Giri a sinistra! = Turn left! (formal / singular)
- Gira a destra! = Turn right! (informal / singular)
- Girate in Via Dante! = Turn on Dante Street (plural)

H

When 'h' begins a word, it's silent.
→ hotel = hotel (oh·tel)

When 'h' combines with 'c' or 'g', it gives them a hard sound.
→ chi = who (kee)
→ laghi = lakes (lah·gee)

Verbs

avere = to have
(io) **ho** = I have (oh)
(tu) **hai** = You have (ah·ee)
(lui/lei) **ha** = He/she has (ah)
(Lei) **ha** = You (formal) have
(loro) **hanno** = They have (ahn·no)

'Avere' only has 2 conjugations that begin with 'a' - the rest begin with 'h'.

• Ho 43 anni. = I'm 43 years old.
• Abbiamo bisogno di dormire. = We need to sleep.
• Hai sete. = You're thirsty.
• Lei ha una figlia? = Do you (formal) have a daughter?

See letter 'A' for more phrases that go with 'avere'.

64

I

Sounds like `ee`

The preposition `a` can also mean `at`, `in` or `to`. See letter `A`!

Words + Phrases

- Io = I

- In = In / At | To | By | On
Use `in` with geographical locations larger than a city:
  → In Italia = In / To Italy

..with certain places in the city:
  → In chiesa = In / To / At church
  → In centro = In / To downtown

..with most methods of transportation using the verb `andare` (to go):
  → In autobus = By bus
  → In treno = By train
  → In macchina = By car
  → In bicicletta = By bike
  → In metropolitana = By subway
  → In aeroplano = By airplane

..with street names to mean `on`:
  → **In** Via Dante = On Dante Street

Il conto, per favore.
=
The bill, please.

(Typically, you must ask for the bill when you're ready to leave the restaurant.)

- Ieri = Yesterday
- Insieme = Together
- Infatti = In fact, indeed
- Immediatamente = Immediately
- Invece = Instead
- Inutile = Useless
- Intorno = Around
- Interno = Inside
- Intero = Whole, entire
- Indietro = Behind (Use interchangeably with `dietro`.)
- In orario = On time
- In anticipo = Early
- In ritardo = Late
- In bocca al lupo = Good luck / Break a leg

Expressions of time

literally: `in the mouth of the wolf`!

65

I

(I')• iogurt = yogurt
(I')• indirizzo = address
(I')• idea = idea (pronounced `ee·day·ah')
(I')• isola = island
(I')• inverno = Winter
(I')• incrocio = intersection
(I')• isolato = city block
(I')• inizio = beginning
(I')• invito = invitation
(I')• ingresso = entrance
(I')• intenzione = intention
(I')• incidente = accident
(I')• illusione = illusion
(I')• imbarco = loading, boarding
(I')• immagine = Image
(I')• insalata = salad (Italian salads are simple, usually consisting of lettuce, olive oil and vinegar. They're served after the main course)
(I')• incontro = a meeting (encounter)

There are various ways to indicate meeting up with others:

→ **Un incontro** (A meeting as an encounter)

→ **Un appuntamento** (An appointment or date)

→ **Una riunione** (A gathering or meeting)

Verbs

1) incontrare = to meet up with someone **(R)**

(io) incontro   (noi) incontriamo
(tu) incontri   (voi) incontrate
(lui/lei incontra   (loro) incontrano
  Lei)

Remember, you can use the present tense to depict the near future.

• Incontro Gianni in centro.
  I'll meet Gianni downtown.

66

I

2) indossare = to wear **(R)**

(io) indosso   (noi) indossiamo
(tu) indossi   (voi) indossate
(lui/lei   indossa   (loro) indossano
Lei)

'Mettersi' = 'to put on'
'Vestirsi' = to get dressed
Both are reflexive.

'Portare' (R) also means 'to wear!'

L'abbigliamento / I vestiti = clothing

- la camicia = shirt
- la camicetta = blouse
- la maglietta / il T-shirt = T-shirt
- il maglione = sweater
- la felpa = sweatshirt
- la giacca = jacket
- il cappotto = coat
- l'impermeabile = raincoat
- i pantaloni = pants
- i jeans = jeans
- i pantaloncini = shorts
- la gonna = skirt
- il vestito = dress / suit
- i calzini = socks
- le scarpe = shoes
  - da tennis = tennis shoes
- gli stivali = boots
- i sandali = sandals
- il cappello = hat
- gli occhiali = glasses
  - da sole = sunglasses
- il costume da bagno = swimsuit
- la borsa = bag / purse

Lei indossa la gonna viola e gialla, e la camicia bianca.
(She's wearing a purple and yellow skirt and a white shirt.)

Anche porta il cappello, la borsa, e gli stivali marrone.
(She's also wearing a brown hat, bag and boots.)

L

Words + Phrases

- Lui = He
- Lei = She / You (formal)

when written, You formal is usually capitalized.

- Loro = They / The possessive pronoun, 'their'
- Là = There
- Lì = There

'Lì' usually refers to something closer than 'là', and more specific

- Leggero = Light (in substance)
- Lento = Slow
- Lentamente = Slowly
- Liscio = Smooth

Many adjectives (lento) like can be converted to adverbs (lentamente) by adding -mente to the end.

Make sure to * change the adjective to its singular feminine form first

- Rapido → Rapidamente
- Certo → Certamente
- Assoluto → Assolutamente

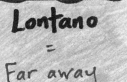

Lontano = Far away (To ask if something is far away, say **È lontano?**)

Nouns

- luglio = July
- (il) lunedì = Monday
- (il) luogo = place
- (la) lattuga = lettuce
- (il) limoncello = lemon flavored digestivo
- (il) latte = milk
  (Remember to order 'caffè latte' if you want espresso with milk.)
- (la) latteria = dairy shop
- (la) libreria = bookstore
- (il) libro = book
- (il) lavoro = work / job

- (la) lavatrice = washing machine
- (la) lavapiatti / lavastoviglie = dishwasher
- (la) lavanderia = laundromat / room
- (la) lampada = lamp
- (la) luce = light
- (il) letto = bed
  (camera da letto = bedroom)
- (il) lenzuolo = sheet (on a bed)
- (la) lana = wool
- (la) luna = moon
- (il) lago = lake
  (Remember to add an 'h' in the plural form → 'laghi')

L

Loro - Possessive Pronoun

'Loro' is also a subject pronoun (they), but here we will discuss 'loro' as a possessive pronoun meaning 'their'.

Remember, when indicating possession, include the definite article of the noun.

(il loro libro = their book (masculine, singular)

(i loro libri = their books (masculine, plural)

(la loro casa = their house (feminine, singular)

(le loro case = their houses (feminine, plural)

'Loro' is the only possessive pronoun that will not change forms. Make sure to modify the article and end of the noun however, when changing from singular to plural.

With all of the other possessive pronouns (see letters 'M', 'N', 'S', 'T' and 'V') you won't include the definite article when talking about a family member in the singular. With 'loro', however, you do!

→ il loro figlio = their son

→ la loro figlia = their daughter

L

'Lasciami stare' = Leave me alone

Verbs

1) lasciare = to leave something **(R)**

(io) lascio	(noi) lasciamo
(tu) lasci	(voi) lasciate
(lui/lei/Lei) lascia	(loro) lasciano

- Mi lasci la chiave? = You'll leave the key for me?
- Lasciamo una mancia. = We're leaving a tip.

There is a cover charge included in the restaurant bill, but you can still leave a tip if you want, even though it's not expected.

2) leggere = to read **(R)**

Remember the 2 different sounds of the 'g' depending on what vowel follows.

(io) leggo	(noi) leggiamo
(tu) leggi	(voi) leggete
(lui/lei/Lei) legge	(loro) leggono

- Leggono il giornale. = They're reading the newspaper.
- Leggete molti libri. = You all read many books.

3) lavare = to wash **(R)**

Contrast with the verb, 'lavarsi' = to wash oneself.

(io) lavo	(noi) laviamo
(tu) lavi	(voi) lavate
(lui/lei/Lei) lava	(loro) lavano

- Lavo i piatti. = I'm washing the dishes.
- Mi lavo. = I'm washing myself.

The verb **'lavorare'** = to work. Conjugate on your own!

Remember! 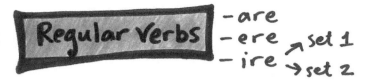 Regular Verbs

-are
-ere → set 1
-ire → set 2

By now, you have seen many regular verbs, all noted in this book with (R); The -are group being the largest.

When you conjugate a regular verb, simply remove the -are, -ere or -ire ending, and replace with a formula. The formula is very similar between all 3 groups, the -ere & -ire (set1) conjugations being almost identical.

-are

(io) - o   (noi) - iamo
(tu) - i   (voi) - ate
(lui/lei/Lei) - a (loro) - ano

mang~~iare~~ = to eat

(Io) mang<u>io</u> = I eat
                    I'm eating
                    I do eat

-ere

(io) - o   (noi) - iamo
(tu) - i   (voi) - ete
(lui/lei/Lei) - e (loro) - ono

prend~~ere~~ = to take

(Lui) prend<u>e</u> = He takes
                     He's taking
                     He does take

-ire (set 1)

(io) - o   (noi) - iamo
(tu) - i   (voi) - ite
(lui/lei/Lei) - e (loro) - ono

dorm~~ire~~ = to sleep

(Loro) dorm<u>ono</u> = They sleep
                       They're sleeping
                       They do sleep

-ire (set 2)

(io) - isco   (noi) - iamo
(tu) - isci   (voi) - ite
(lui/lei/Lei) - isce (loro) - iscono

cap~~ire~~ = to understand

(Tu) cap <u>isci</u> = You understand
                      You're understanding
                      You do understand

Words + Phrases

• Molto = Many / Very / A lot

When 'molto' describes a noun, it means 'many' and its ending will agree with the noun:
→ Molte persone = Many people
→ Molti pomodori = Many tomatoes

When 'molto' describes an adjective, it means 'very' and will remain unmodified:
→ Sono molto divertenti. = They're very fun.

When 'molto' describes a verb, it means 'a lot' and also remains unmodified:
→ Viaggiano molto. = They travel a lot.

• Male = Badly / Poorly
An adverb that will describe a verb.
→ Canto male. = I sing poorly.

• Mi piacerebbe = It would please me
Use with singular nouns and verbs.
→ Mi piacerebbe mangiare.
(Eating would please me.)
→ Mi piacerebbe un gelato.
(An ice cream would please me.)

• Mi piacerebbero = They'd please me.
Use with plural nouns.
→ Mi piacerebbero le nuove scarpe.
(The new shoes would please me.)

Mille grazie!
=
A thousand thanks!

(You can also say,
→ Molto grazie!
→ Molte grazie!
or
→ Grazie mille!
→ Grazie molto!)

(The 'molto' meaning 'many' or 'a lot!)

• Migliore = Best
• Mammamia! = Oh my!
• Madonna! = Oh my goodness!
• Mannaggia! = Dangit!
• Mi manchi = I miss you

• Ma = But
• Magari = Perhaps
• Meno = Less
• Meglio = Better

72

M

The 'mi' is an indirect object pronoun. See grammar section and the letter 'P' for more on piacere.

- Mi piace = It's pleasing to me.
  - → Mi piace il quadro. = The painting is pleasing to me.
  - → Mi piace ballare. = Dancing is pleasing to me.
- Mi piacciono = They're pleasing to me.
  - → Mi piacciono i vestiti. = The clothes are pleasing to me.
- Mai = Never
  ↓
  To say you never do something, begin with 'Non' + conjugated verb + 'mai'.
  - → Lui non chiama mai. = He never calls.
- Mio = Mine (Possessive pronoun, see below)

Mio

- il mio passaporto = my passport (singular, masculine)
- i miei occhiali = my glasses   (plural, masculine)
- la mia borsa = my bag (singular, feminine)
- le mie chiavi = my keys (plural, feminine)

Remember that the form of 'mio' is based on the object being possessed and not the possessor of the object.

With family members, drop the article in the singular form.

(singular) mia sorella = my sister   but le mie sorelle (plural)
           mio fratello = my brother   i miei fratelli

* I miei fratelli can refer to my brothers or my siblings.

73

M

To put on clothing, use `mettersi` as a reflexive verb. See grammar section.

1) mettere = to put / place **(R)**

(io) metto   (noi) mettiamo
(tu) metti   (voi) mettete
(lui/lei mette   (loro) mettono
Lei)

- Mettiamo i piatti sulla tavola. = We're putting the plates on the table.
- Metto il cellulare nella borsa. = I'm putting the cell phone in the bag.

2) mangiare = to eat **(R)**

(io) mangio   (noi) mangiamo
(tu) mangi   (voi) mangiate
(lui/lei mangia   (loro) mangiano
Lei)

- Mangiate a mezzogiorno. = You all eat at noon.
- Lei mangia lentamente. = You (formal) eat slowly.
- Mangiamo! = Let's eat (command form - see grammar section)

Italy is a country renown for its simple and delicious cuisine. Each of the 20 regions specializes in different foods which ensures that no matter where you go, you will eat well: various pastas, `risotto`, `polenta`, `pizza`, fresh bread, cured meats, `parmigiano`, `ricotta`, `gelato`, `espresso`, and delectable wines. Fresh and artisanal, with attention to detail and subtleties of flavor - these aspects are the cornerstone of Italian food. Buon appetito!

M

Mangiare

A tavola
(At the table)

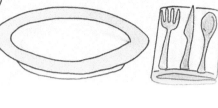

- il piatto = plate
- la scodella = bowl
- il bicchiere = glass
- la forchetta = fork
- il coltello = knife
- il cucchiaio = spoon
  (koo-kee-eye-oh)
  → cucchiaino = little spoon
  → cucchiaione = big spoon
- la tovaglia = table cloth
- il tovagliolo = napkin

> -ino on the end of a noun makes it smaller, while -one makes it bigger.

I piatti
(The courses)

> The word for 'plate' and 'course' is the same.

- l'antipasto = appetizer
- il primo = the first course (grains)
- il secondo = the second course (protein)
- il contorno = the vegetables
  > comes after the main dish
- il dolce = dessert
- le bevande / bibite = drinks
  → l'acqua (naturale o frizzante) = water
    ↓ still   ↓ bubbly
  → il vino = wine (rosso o bianco)
    ↓ red   ↓ white
  → il digestivo = hard alcohol consumed after the meal

In Italy, the drink called 'l'aperitivo' is consumed before the meal in order to open one's appetite. It also refers to the time of day (at the end of work), for doing so. In America, we call this time 'Happy Hour'! After the meal, a different type of alcohol is often consumed in order to help digest the food, hence its name, 'il digestivo'. 'L'espresso' is commonly drank after a meal and before 'il digestivo'.

M

Mangiare continued

In bigger cities, you will find many food options for dining out. Otherwise, in typical towns, the main types of places to eat meals at include:

Il bar / caffè → For a light breakfast of a beverage and pastry. Also for a light lunch consisting of a sandwich and beverage.

La pizzeria → Most 'pizzerie' serve just pizza; others include pasta on the menu. Italian pizza has fewer toppings, it is thinner, and you eat it with a fork and knife. 'La pizza margherita' (mozzarella, tomato sauce, basil) is simple and delicious; the best is in Naples!

La paninoteca → 'Panini' are sandwiches. Many 'bar' l'caffè' will have them prepared in a case. When you order, it will be placed in a grill. At the 'paninoteca', you will find a broad variety of sandwiches.

La trattoria → A family owned restaurant that serves food typical of the region. Typically smaller and less expensive than the 'ristorante.'

Il ristorante → Very similar to the 'trattoria', but typically a bit more formal. A service charge is included in the bill (also at the trattoria), so you don't need to leave a tip.

After you eat, you can go to the 'gelateria' for some delicious ice cream

Il conto, per favore.
=
The bill, please.
(Ask for the bill when you're ready to leave the 'trattoria' and 'ristorante.' You can stay as long as you like.)

M

Nouns

- marzo = March
- maggio = May
- (il) • martedì = Tuesday
- (il) • mercoledì = Wednesday
- (la) • mattina = morning
- (il) • mezzogiorno = noon
- (la) • mezzanotte = midnight
- (il) • mese = month
- (la) • macchina = car
- (la) • macchina fotografica = camera
- (il) • motorino = moped
- (la) • motocicletta = motorcycle (abbreviated to 'la moto')
- (la) • metropolitana = subway
- (il) • museo = museum
- (il) • mercato = market
- (la) • macelleria = meat shop
- (il) • mare = sea
- (la) • montagna = mountain
- (il) • medico = doctor
- (il) • mondo = world
- (la) • moneta = coins, change
- (la) • mancia = tip, gratuity
- (la) • marca = brand name
- (il) • miele = honey
- (la) • minestra = soup
- (la) • musica = music
- (la) • mozzarella = In Italy you can find 'mozzarella di bufala' (buffalo) - deliziosa!
- (la) • multa = fine
- (la) • madre = mother
      (mamma = mom)

> The word 'camera' in Italian, means 'room'

> In restaurants, the service charge is factored into the bill, so while the tip is appreciated, it isn't necessary.

> Make sure to validate your bus and train ticket, so you don't get one!

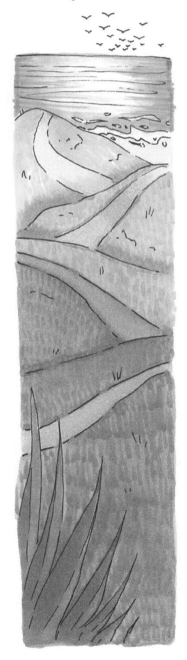

77

N

Non lo so = I don't know

Words + Phrases

- No = No
- Non = Makes a sentence negative and precedes the verb. (eg. Non mangio = I'm not eating).
- Non c'è male = Not bad (Answers the questions 'Come sta?' or 'Come va?')
- Non c'è problema = No problem
- Non ce lo faccio = I can't make it happen
- Non ne ho = I don't have any ('Ne' refers to a quantity)
- Nessuno = Nobody
- Niente / Nulla = Nothing
- Noi = We
- Non si fa così = You don't do it like that. (You may hear this phrase regarding unacceptable behaviors).
- Nostro = Our (Possessive pronoun, see below)

Nostro

- il nostro amico = our friend (male)   (singular, masculine)
- i nostri colleghi = our colleagues   (plural, masculine)
- la nostra professoressa = our professor (female)   (singular, feminine)
- le nostre vicine = our neighbors (female)   (plural, feminine)

And for family:
- → nostro nonno = our grandfather
  - but i nostri nonni = our grandfathers / grandparents

- → nostra nonna = our grandmother
  - but le nostre nonne = our grandmothers

N

Nouns

- novembre = November
- (il) · negozio = store
- (la) · neve = snow
- (la) · nebbia = fog
- (la) · nuvola = cloud

- (il) · nord = North
- (la) · notte = night
- (la) · nave = ship
- (la) · nocciola = hazelnut
- (il) · numero = number

Numbers

1	2	3	4	5	6	7	8	9	10
uno	due	tre	quattro	cinque	sei	sette	otto	nove	dieci

11	12	13	14	15	16	17	18	19	20
undici	dodici	tredici	quattordici	quindici	sedici	diciassette	diciotto	diciannove	venti

30 = trenta
40 = quaranta
50 = cinquanta
60 = sessanta
70 = settanta
80 = ottanta
90 = novanta
100 = cento
1.000 = mille
5.000 = cinquemila
100.000 = centomila
1.000.000 = un milione

↑ Use decimal points instead of a comma.

Drop the vowel before 'uno' and 'otto'

Add an accent to the 'e' in tre when it's attached to another number

21 = ventuno
32 = trentadue
43 = quarantatré
54 = cinquantaquattro
65 = sessantacinque
76 = settantasei
87 = ottantasette
98 = novantotto
109 = centonove
223 = duecentoventitré
2019 = duemiladiciannove

Use 'mille' only for one thousand, and 'mila' for two thousand and up.

Verbs

1) noleggiare = to rent (R)

(io) noleggio   (noi) noleggiamo
(tu) noleggi   (voi) noleggiate
(lui/lei   noleggia   (loro) noleggiano
 Lei)

- Noleggiamo una macchina. = We're renting a car.
- Noleggi quel film? = Are you renting that movie?

'Affittare' (R) also means 'to rent' but in reference to a house or apartment, whereas 'noleggiare' is used for an object like a car, bike, movie, etc.

2) nuotare = to swim (R)

(io) nuoto   (noi) nuotiamo
(tu) nuoti   (voi) nuotate
(lui/lei nuota   (loro) nuotano
 Lei)

- Lui nuota ogni mattina. = He swims every morning.
- Nuotano anche in inverno. = They also swim in the winter.

Usually 'nuotare' refers to swimming as a sport and 'fare un bagno' means 'to take a dip.'

- O = Or
- Oppure = Or, otherwise
- Ogni = Each, every
- Ognuno = Each one
- Oggi = Today
- Ovviamente = Obviously
- Occhio! = Look out!
- Ohi! = Hey!
- Ormai = By now

Ora di cena
=
Dinnertime

(You can follow the phrase, 'Ora di...' with a noun or verb to indicate that it's time for that thing.)

→ **Ora di dormire**
=
Time to sleep

The letter 'O' has 2 different sounds:
→ An open 'oh' sound like in the word 'oggi'
or
→ A closed 'oh' sound as in the word 'ora'.
A double 'oo' is pronounced like 'oh'!

- Ora = Now

Nouns

- ottobre = October
- (l') ospedale = hospital
- (l') orto = vegetable garden
- (l') orso = bear
- (l') ovest = West
- (l') orologio = clock/watch
- (l') ombra = shade
- (l') ombrello = umbrella
- (gli) occhiali = glasses

- (l') ora = hour, time
- (le) olive = olives
- (l') olio d'oliva = olive oil
- (l') ospite = host/hostess/guest
- (l') onda = wave (in the ocean)
- (l') oceano = ocean
- (l') oro = gold
- (l') orario = schedule
- (l') orizzonte = horizon

 Telling time

Che ora è?
Che ore sono? = What time is it? The question is asked in either the singular or plural form because the hour is either singular or plural.

Answer in the singular form for the following times:

→ È mezzogiorno. = It's noon.

→ È mezzanotte. = It's midnight.

→ È l'una. = It's **1**.00 (Use a period instead of a colon for time.)

Answer in the plural form for any other time:

→ Sono le due. = It's 2.00.

→ Sono le cinque. = It's 5.00.

→ Sono le undici. = It's 11.00.

← These hours are greater than 1, which is why they're written in the plural form.

To add minutes to any time singular or plural, simply say and = e.

→ Sono le sei e dieci. = It's 6.10.

→ È l'una e venticinque. = Its 1.25.

The 24 hour clock, or military time, is used often, especially when making official appointments and with the train schedule. Simply add 12 to any time after noon and before midnight.

→ Sono le ventuno e cinque. = 21.05 = 9:05 pm

→ Sono le quindici e venti. = 15.20 = 3:20 pm

Use a number for minutes, or for these following times, you can also use these phrases:

- un quarto = a quarter (past)
- mezzo/a = half (past)
- meno un quarto = minus a quarter

When it's three quarters past the hour and beyond, use 'meno' (minus) to indicate the time. Simply say the hour it will soon be, minus however many minutes are left.

→ Sono le undici meno dieci. = 10.50

→ Sono le due e un quarto. = 2.15
→ Sono le tre e mezzo. = 3.30
→ Sono le cinque meno un quarto. = 4.45

A che ora..? = At what time..?

Ask to find out when certain things are taking place.

Use the singular for the following times:

→ A mezzogiorno. = At noon.
→ A mezzanotte. = At midnight.
→ All'una. = At 1.00.

Use the plural for any other time.

→ Alle due. = At 2.00
→ Alle sei. = At 6.00
→ Alle dieci. = At 10.00

The same rules apply here in regards to singular and plural as when answering the question, 'Che ora è? 'Che ore sono?'

83

Ora

Some good questions to remember:

→ A che ora parte il treno? = At what time does the train depart?

→ A che ora arriva l'autobus? = At what time does the bus arrive?

→ A che ora apre il ristorante? = At what time does the restaurant open?

→ A che ora chiude il negozio? = At what time does the store close?

Indicate the time of day either by using the 24 hour clock or by using these phrases for times of day:

- di mattina = in the morning
- del pomeriggio = in the afternoon
- di sera = in the evening
- di notte = at night

→ Sono le nove e cinque di mattina. = 9.05

→ È l'una e mezzo del pomeriggio. = 13.30

→ Sono le sei e dieci di sera. = 18.10

→ Sono le undici meno un quarto di sera. = 22.45

→ Sono le tre e trentacinque di notte. = 3.35

'Tempo' can be used to refer to a quantity of time.
→ Quanto tempo ci vuole? = How much time does it take?
Otherwise, 'tempo' refers to weather (letters 'C', 'F,')
'T'

Non vedo l'ora! = I can't wait!
L'ora di cena. = Dinner time.
← Good phrases to know.

Verbs

1) ordinare = to order (request, command)
to organize **(R)**

(io) ordino	(noi) ordiniamo
(tu) ordini	(voi) ordinate
(lui/lei ordina	(loro) ordinano
Lei)	

The verb 'prendere' is more commonly used when ordering food

- Ordiniamo qualcosa! = Let's order something!
- Il professore ci ordina di fare i compiti.
  = The professor orders us to do our homework.
- Metto in ordine la casa. = I'm organizing the house.

(a phrase; 'in order')

2) offrire = to offer **(R)**

(io) offro	(noi) offriamo
(tu) offri	(voi) offrite
(lui/lei offre	(loro) offrono
Lei)	

- Offro un caffè alla mia amica. = I'm offering a coffee to my friend.
- Il bar offre molte scelte. = The coffee shop offers many choices.

85

P

- Piacere. = Pleased to meet you. Also the verb, 'to be pleasing!'
- Permesso? = Permission? (Can I?)
- Per favore = Please
- Penso di sì. = I think so.
- Penso di no. = I think not.
- Perché? = Why? (Also, 'Because').
- Presto = Soon ('A presto!' = See you soon.)
- Per = For
- Pronto = Ready (Italians say this when answering the phone.
- Poi = Then, next
- Poco → As an adjective it means 'few' and is modified to agree with the noun. As an adverb it means 'a little' and is unmodified.

→ C'è poca gente. = There are few people.
→ Corre poco. = He runs a little.

- Parecchio = Many / A lot

As an adjective it means, and agrees with the noun.

As an adverb it means, and doesn't agree.

→ Hai parecchi libri. = You have many books.
→ Studi parecchio. = You study a lot.

- Però = But
- Prossimo = Next
- Purtroppo = Unfortunately
- Probabilmente = Probably
- Perfetto = Perfect
- Piccante = Spicy
- Più = More
- Più o meno = More or less

Prego.
=
You're welcome.

(Also use it to get someone's attention, to ask 'what?' or to express allowance.)

→ **Prego?** = What? Excuse me?

→ **Prego.** = Go ahead.

- Peggio = Worse
- Peggiore = Worst
- Peccato = A pity
  Also means 'a sin!'

Peccato!
or
Che peccato!
= Too bad, what a pity!

86

P

The letter 'P' begins many important Italian words (parole). Just think of the most popular (più popolare) foods - pasta, pizza, panini, parmigiana, pane!

(la) • primavera = Spring
(il) • primo piatto = first course
(il) • panino = sandwich
(la) • pasta = pastry/dough/pasta
(la) • pasticceria = pastry shop
(la) • panetteria/panificio = bread shop
(la) • piazza = town square/plaza (integral to Italian life 'in centro')
(la) • polizia = police
(il) • ponte = bridge
(il) • paese = country/village
(il) • paio = pair
(il) • parco = park
(la) • parola = word
(il) • passaporto = passport
(il) • pavimento = the floor

(il) • pomeriggio = afternoon
(il) • pane = bread
(la) • pizza = ☺
(il) • pasto = meal
(la) • paninoteca = sandwich shop
(la) • pizzeria = pizza parlor
(i) • peperoni = bell peppers
(la) • porta = door
(il) • palazzo = building
(la) • pace = peace
(il/la) • parente = relative
(la) • partenza = departure
(la) • pausa = a break
(il) • pranzo = lunch

(il) • piano = floor (of a building) → in Italy 'pianterreno' is the ground floor, 'primo piano' is the 2nd floor, 'secondo piano' = 3rd floor

(il) • prezzo = price
(la) • persona = person
(la) • piscina = pool

(la) • pioggia = rain
(il) • pezzo = piece
(la) • pianta = plant

87

P

Nouns

(il) • pomodoro = tomato

(la) • pera = pear

(il) • peperoncino = chili pepper

(la) • polenta = polenta

(la) • piadina = A flat bread filled with meat and or cheese.

(la) • poltrona = armchair

(la) • posta = mail

(la) • pelle = skin

(il) • papà = dad

(il) • papa = The Pope

(la) • pappa = baby food

Note the similarities between these 3 words

(il) • padre = father

(la) • pesca = peach / fishing

→ Mangio una pesca.
   = I'm eating a peach.

→ Andiamo a pesca.
   = We're going fishing.

Verbs

1) prendere = to take / get **(R)**

(io) prendo

(tu) prendi

(lui/lei Lei) prende

(noi) prendiamo

(voi) prendete

(loro) prendono

'Prendere' is used literally in some ways, e.g. 'to take a train', or 'to get' an object. It's also used idiomatically when ordering food. Many translations of 'to take' however use the verb 'fare' instead. See letter F.

• Prendo un cappuccino. = I'm getting a cappuccino.

• Prendete l'autobus. = You all are taking the bus.

• Lei prende i ravioli? = Are you (formal) getting ravioli?

P

Review 'indirect object pronouns' and 'disjunctive pronouns' in the grammar section.

2) **piacere** = to be pleasing (I)

(io) piaccio   (noi) piacciamo
(tu) piaci   (voi) piacete
(lui/lei **piace**)   * (loro) **piacciono**
Lei)

*The most commonly used conjugations.

Use with singular nouns and verbs.

Use with plural nouns.

In English we say we 'like' something or someone, but in Italian you say the thing/person that's liked is pleasing to a person/people. Therefore, you must use an indirect object pronoun or disjunctive pronoun (with 'a') in order to form phrases with 'piacere'!

With indirect object pronouns:

→ Mi piace ballare. = Dancing is pleasing to me.
→ Le piacciono i fiori. = Flowers are pleasing to her/you formal.
→ Ci piace la macchina. = The car is pleasing to us.

With disjunctive pronouns:

→ A te piace sciare. = Skiing is pleasing to you.
→ A voi piacciono gli stivali. = Boots are pleasing to you all.
→ A loro piace il tiramisù. = Tiramisù is pleasing to them.

If you want to say 'I like you', you say 'You are pleasing to me' → Mi piaci.

P `piacere` continued

If you want to use a person's name instead of a pronoun, simply put `a` in front of the name, the correct form of `piacere`, and finally, the verb or noun(s).

- A Sofia piace il gelato. = Ice cream is pleasing to Sofia.
- A Lucia e Franco piace lavorare. = Working is pleasing to Lucia and Franco.
- A Marta piace cucinare. = Cooking is pleasing to Marta.

When you want to say that something is not pleasing, place **`non`** in front of the indirect object pronoun.

With indirect object pronouns :

→ Non mi piace pulire. = Cleaning isn't pleasing to me.

→ Non ci piacciono i peperoni. = Bell peppers aren't pleasing to us.

→ Non vi piace quel corso. = That class isn't pleasing to you all.

When using a disjunctive pronoun or someone's name, place **`non`** in front of the conjugation of `piacere`!

With disjunctive pronouns and names :

→ A te non piace alzarti presto. = Getting up early isn't pleasing to you.

→ A Stella non piace lavare i piatti. = cleaning dishes isn't pleasing to Stella.

P

3) potere = to be able to / can (I)

(io) posso   (noi) possiamo
(tu) puoi   (voi) potete
(lui/lei Lei) può   (loro) possono

'Potere', 'dovere' (see letter 'D') and 'volere' (see letter 'V'), are called modal verbs. They're all used frequently. If another verb follows, conjugate the modal verb and leave the second verb in its infinitive.

- Puoi venire con me? = Can you come with me?
- Lui può fare un viaggio. = He's able to take a trip.

You can use 'potere' to ask if you can do something, see or touch something, and so forth.

⤳ Posso? = Can I?
⤳ Possiamo? = Can we?

P

Verbs

4) preferire = to prefer (R) — -ire set 2

(io) preferisco   (noi) preferiamo
(tu) preferisci   (voi) preferite
(lui/lei / Lei) preferisce   (loro) preferiscono

> You can follow 'preferire' with another verb or a noun. Just like with the modal verbs or any verb phrase (two consecutive verbs), conjugate 'preferire' and leave the second verb in the infinitive form.

- Preferisco prendere il tè. = I prefer to get (the) tea.
- Preferiscono la pasta al dente. = They prefer pasta cooked slightly firm.

5) partire = to depart (R) — -ire set 1

> Use 'partire' to leave a city.

(io) parto   (noi) partiamo
(tu) parti   (voi) partite
(lui/lei / Lei) parte   (loro) partono

- Partite domani. = You all are leaving tomorrow.
- Partiamo fra 2 giorni. = We're leaving in 2 days.

The verb **'pensare'** means → **to think**. It's regular **(R)**.
To say you're thinking of doing something, follow 'pensare' with 'di' → **Penso di studiare.** = I'm thinking of studying.
To say you're thinking of a person, follow 'pensare' with 'a'!
→ **Pensi a me?** = Are you thinking of me?
Be careful using verbs like 'pensare', 'credere' (to believe) and 'immaginare' (to imagine)! Among many other verbs and phrases, they express something imagined or wished and require a different verb tense not taught in this book.

P

> 'Per' is included in the verb's definition.

6) pagare = to pay for (R)

(io) pago	(noi) paghiamo
(tu) paghi	(voi) pagate
(lui/lei Lei) paga	(loro) pagano

- Pago la cena. = I'm paying for dinner.
- Paghiamo noi. = We're paying. ← The subject pronoun at the end shows emphasis.

7) portare = to carry / bring / wear (R)

(io) porto	(noi) portiamo
(tu) porti	(voi) portate
(lui/lei Lei) porta	(loro) portano

- Porti due valige. = You're carrying two suitcases.
- Portate l'acqua? = Are you all bringing water?
- Portano gli stivali rossi. = They're wearing red boots.

8) parlare = to speak/talk (R)

(io) parlo	(noi) parliamo
(tu) parli	(voi) parlate
(lui/lei Lei) parla	(loro) parlano

If you follow 'parlare' with 'a' it means you're talking 'to'.
→ Parlo a Donatella. = I'm speaking to Donatella.
If you follow 'parlare' with 'di' it means you're talking 'about.'
→ Parliamo di politica. = We're speaking about politics.

93

Q

Words + Phrases

- Quanto/a? = How much?
- Quanti/e? = How many?

If 'quanto' is followed by a noun, the ending will agree.
- → Quanti pomodori? = How many tomatoes?
- → Quante persone? = How many people?

- Quale/i? = Which

'Quale' refers to anything singular, and 'quali', to plural things.
- → Quale casa? = Which house?
- → Quali scarpe? = Which shoes?

'Q' is always followed by 'u' and sounds like 'kw'
- → Qui = Kwee

- Quando? = When?
- Qui
- Qua
= Here

'Qui technically refers to something precisely 'here', while 'qua' can mean nearby in proximity.

Quanto costa?
=
How much does it cost?

(If the items are plural, say → **Quanto costano?**)

- Qualcosa = Something
- Qualcuno = Someone
- Qualche = Few, some
- Qualsiasi = Any
- Quasi = Almost
- Quindi = Therefore
- Questo/a = This
- Questi/e = These

The form changes with the noun it modifies.

- → Questa mela = This apple
- → Queste mele = These apples
- → Questo sugo = This sauce
- → Questi sughi = These sauces

94

• Quello = That

'Quello', like 'bello', has 8 different forms when it comes before a noun.

Quello + il = **Quel** bambino = That little boy

lo = **Quello** studente = That (male) student

l' = **Quell'** amico = That (male) friend

i = **Quei** bambini = Those little boys

gli = **Quegli** studenti = Those students

amici = Those friends

la = **Quella** ragazza = That girl

l' = **Quell'** amica = That (female) friend

le = **Quelle** ragazze = Those girls

amiche = Those (girl) friends

The plural forms of 'quello,'
→ quei
→ quegli
→ quelle
mean 'those'

Nouns

(il) • quadro = painting
(il) • quartiere = district
(la) • questione = question / issue
(il) • quarto = a quarter
        (used in time)

R

- Ripeta, per favore ! = Repeat, please! **(F)**
- (Ha) ragione. = You're right. **(F)**
  * Use any conjugation of 'avere' before 'ragione'!
- (Che) ridere ! = How funny!
- (Mi) raccamondo = I advise you
- (In) ritardo = Late
- Rapido = Fast

Nouns

(la) • risata = laugh
(il) • ristorante = restaurant
(i) • ravioli = stuffed pasta
(il) • riso = rice
(il) • risotto = a creamy rice dish
(la) • riunione = a meeting/ gathering
(la) • ruota = wheel
(la) • roba = stuff
(il) • rumore = noise
(la) • roccia = rock
(la) • rivista = magazine
(il) • regalo = gift
(il) • rasoio = razor
(il) • ricordo = a memory
(il) • ritorno = return
(il) • ragazzo = boy
(la) • ragazza = girl

(la) • richiesta = request
(la) • radio = radio
(il) • ragno = spider
(la) • rana = frog
(la) • ricetta = recipe
(la?) risposta = response
(il) • riposo = rest

'Ragazzo/a' can also be used to mean 'boyfriend' or 'girlfriend'.

(il) • ricordino = souvenir

When buying a round trip train ticket, say 'Andata e ritorno, per favore').

(i) ragazzi = boys, or boys and girls

(le) ragazze = girls

(il) • Rinascimento = The Renaissance

R

1) restare = to stay/remain **(R)**

(io) resto   (noi) restiamo
(tu) resti   (voi) restate
(lui/lei resta   (loro) restano
   Lei)

- Resti a casa? = Are you staying at home?
- Restano a Roma adesso. = They're staying in Rome now.

2) ridere = to laugh **(R)**

(io) rido   (noi) ridiamo
(tu) ridi   (voi) ridete
(lui/lei ride   (loro) ridono
   Lei)

- Rido sempre. = I always laugh.
- Che ridere! = How funny!

> See grammar section in beginning of book on Reflexive verbs

3) riposarsi = to rest oneself **(R)**

> Remember to include the reflexive pronoun in front of the conjugation

(io) <u>mi</u> riposo   (noi) <u>ci</u> riposiamo
(tu) <u>ti</u> riposi   (voi) <u>vi</u> riposate
(lui/lei <u>si</u> riposa   (loro) <u>si</u> riposano
   Lei)

- Ci riposiamo sul divano. = We're resting on the couch.
- Vi riposate facilmente. = You all relax easily.

Another reflexive verb similar in meaning to 'riposarsi', is '**rilassarsi**' = to relax oneself **(R)**. See if you can conjugate it on your own.

(io) _____   (noi) _____
(tu) _____   (voi) _____
(lui/lei/Lei) _____   (loro) _____

S

• Sí = Yes

Si (without a written accent) can be placed in front of the 'lui/lei' or 'loro' conjugations to indicate the following:

1) A reflexive pronoun.
→ Si alza. = He/she gets up.
→ Si alzano. = They get up.

2) A generalized statement about what people do, or a passive construction.
→ Si cena alle otto. = People eat dinner at 8.00.
→ Si parla italiano. = Italian is spoken.
→ Si vendono i biglietti. = Tickets are sold.

3) A way to express 'you' or 'we.'
→ Come si dice? = How do you say?
→ Che si fa oggi? = What are we doing today?

Only use the 'lui/lei' form here

Scusi? (F)
=
Excuse me?
(Use to get a person's attention or ask a question).
→ **Scusi, signora?**
(Excuse me, ma'am)
→ **Scusi, Signore?**
(Excuse me, sir)

• Salute! = Cheers!
• Salve = Hello / Goodbye (Formal version of 'ciao'). **(F)**
• Signora = Ma'am, Mrs.
• Signore = Sir, Mr.
• Signorina = Miss
• Sto bene = I'm well.
  .. male = I'm not well.

Answers the question, 'Come sta?' **(F)**

• Spero di sí = I hope so
• Sempre = Always
• Sempre dritto = Straight ahead
• Spesso = Often
• Subito = Right away
• Suo = His / Hers/ Yours (formal)

Spero di no. = I hope not.
Speriamo! = Let's hope!

Possessive pronoun – see next pages.

98

S

- Stamattina = This morning
- Stasera = This evening
- Stanotte = Last night → During the night, while people sleep..
- Sogni d'oro = Sweet dreams (dreams of gold)
- Su = On / Up
- Sotto = Under
- Sopra = Above
- (Di) solito = Usually
- Scorso = Last ↘

When 's' begins a word, or is in the middle of a vowel and consonant, it has a soft sound (e.g. sweet). When it's in the middle of 2 vowels, the sound is hard (e.g. zero)

'Scorso' is an adjective, and will agree with the noun it's describing to express a timeframe in the past.

→ la settimana scorsa = last week
→ il mese scorso = last month
→ l'anno scorso = last year

But if you describe a timeframe with a specific number, use 'fa' = ago. ↘

→ dieci minuti fa = 10 minutes ago
→ due ore fa = 2 hours ago
→ tre giorni fa = 3 days ago

You can sometimes use 'scorso' and 'fa' interchangeably.

- la settimana scorsa = una settimana fa
- il mese scorso = un mese fa
- l'anno scorso = un anno fa

S

When 'sc' is combined, it has 2 different sounds.

➜ If followed by 'e' or 'i', it sounds like 'sh':
- sciare = to ski (she·ar·ay)
- scemo = fool (shay·moh)

➜ It followed by 'a', 'o', 'u' or 'h', it sounds like 'sk':
- scala = stair (skah·lah)
- schiena = back (skee·ay·nah)

Suo → Your is you formal

- il suo motorino = his/her/your moped   (singular, masculine)
- i suoi pattini = his/her/your skates   (plural, masculine)
- la sua bicicletta = his/her/your bicycle   (singular, feminine)
- le sue macchine = his/her/your cars   (plural, feminine)

Remember that the form of 'suo' agrees with the object being possessed rather than the possessor of the object.

e.g.➜ La sua bicicletta = Can refer to a guy's bike or a girl's bike or if you're talking to someone in a formal context, 'your bike'!

And for family:
- ➜ sua madre = his/her/your mother
- **but** le sue madri = his/her/your mothers
- ➜ suo padre = his/her/your father
- **but** i suoi padri = his/her/your fathers

The word for 'parents' is 'i genitori'

100

S

- settembre = September
- (il) • sabato = Saturday
- (il) • sole = sun
- (la) • settimana = week
- (la) • sinistra = left
- (la) • sera = evening
- (la) • strada = street
- (il) • soggiorno = } living room
- (il) • salotto =
- (la) • sala da pranzo = dining room
- (lo) • scherzo = joke
- (la) • scatola = box
- (il) • santo = Saint
- (lo) • sciopero = strike
- (il) • sale = salt
- (il) • secondo piatto = second course
- (lo) • spuntino = snack
- (il) • spumante = champagne
- (la) • spremuta = fresh squeezed juice
- (le) • scale = stairs
- (lo) • specchio = mirror
- (la) • stanza = room →
- (la) • spazzola = brush
- (la) • spazzola da denti = toothbrush

Even when there's a train strike, there will still be trains running.

'Camera' also means room

- (il) • semaforo = stoplight
- (il) • sud = South
- (la) • stazione = station (train)
- (il) • supermercato = supermarket
- (lo) • stadio = stadium
- (la) • scuola = school
- (i) • soldi = money
- (la) • spesa = expense
- (lo) • spazio = space
- (la) • spazzatura = garbage
- (la) • statua = statue
- (la) • stella = star
- (la) • salute = health
- (il) • saluto = greeting
- (il) • sacco = sack, bag
- (lo) • scontrino = receipt
- (lo) • sconto = discount
- (le) • scarpe = shoes
  → scarpe da tennis = tennis shoes
- (gli) • stivali = boots
- (la) • sciarpa = scarf

The expression 'un sacco' means 'a lot'

101

S

Verbs

'**Ci sentiamo**' means 'we'll hear from each other.' Use as an informal goodbye.

1) sentire = to hear, feel **(R)**

(io) sento   (noi) sentiamo
(tu) senti   (voi) sentite
(lui/lei sente   (loro) sentono
   Lei)

When 'sentire' means 'to feel', it's addressing a physical sensation or emotion.

→ Sento il caldo dal fuoco. = I feel the heat from the fire.
→ Senti gioia quando balli. = You feel joy when you dance.

And of course, 'sentire' also means 'to hear' → Sentiamo la musica. = We hear the music.

Review reflexive verbs in the grammar section

2) sentirsi = to feel **(R)**

(io) mi sento   (noi) ci sentiamo
(tu) ti senti   (voi) vi sentite
(lui/lei si sente   (loro) si sentono
   Lei)

When 'sentirsi' is reflexive, it means 'to feel like.'

• Mi sento bene. = I feel well.
• Come vi sentite oggi? = How do you all feel today?

The verb '**svegliarsi**' = to wake up. Conjugate on your own!

(io) _____   (noi) _____
(tu) _____   (voi) _____
(lui/lei _____   (loro) _____
   Lei)

102

S

stare → how you're doing
to = be → physical location ('to stay')

essere → identity
→ physical location
→ use with adjectives
→ time

> The conjugation of 'essere' will be on the next page. Most of its forms start with 's'.

3) stare (I)

(io) sto   (noi) stiamo
(tu) stai   (voi) state
(lui/lei sta   (loro) stanno
     Lei)

- Come sta? = How are you (formal) doing?
- Sto bene, grazie. = I'm doing well, thanks.
- Stiamo a casa. = We're at home.
- Stanno a Bologna per 2 giorni. = They're in Bologna for 2 days.

`stare` + infinitive = something is about to happen
→ Stai per mangiare. = You're about to eat.
→ State per partire. = You all are about to depart.

Some useful phrases with 'stare':
→ Stammi bene! = Take care! (informal)
→ Sta' attento/a! = Be careful!
→ Sta' tranquillo/a! = Keep calm!

↑ Review the command forms of 'stare' in the grammar section.

> The ending of 'attento' and 'tranquillo' will be modified based on gender and number.

Say `Sono io' to mean, `it's me.'

4) essere (I)

(io) sono   (noi) siamo
(tu) sei   (voi) siete
(lui/lei è   (loro) sono
   Lei)

Use `essere' to:

a) Introduce yourself and others

→ Sono Danielle. = I'm Danielle.

→ Lei è Gina. = She's Gina.

b) Discuss physical location

→ Sei a scuola. = You're at school.

→ Siamo a Torino. = We're in Turin.

c) With descriptive adjectives

→ Lei è simpatica. = She's nice.

→ Siamo divertenti. = We're fun.

Review the section on adjectives in the beginning of the book.

d) Tell time

→ Che ore sono? = What time is it?

→ È mezzogiorno. = It's noon.

→ Sono le due. = Its 2.00

(See letters `A', `C', `E' and `O', for more on time.)

We've already seen that `stare' can also be used for physical location. While they can sometimes be used interchangeably, `stare' will always indicate staying for a longer period of time, such as overnight.

104

Verbs

5) sapere = to know (a fact / how to do something) **(I)**

(io) so   (noi) sappiamo
(tu) sai   (voi) sapete
(lui/lei   sa   (loro) sanno
   Lei)

Whereas 'conoscere' (see letter 'C') refers to knowing a person, or being acquainted with a place, 'sapere' refers to knowledge in a factual sense. To say you know how to do something (**conjugate sapere + infinitive verb.**)

- Lei sa dov'è il mercato? = Do you (formal) know where the market is?
- Sanno sciare. = They know how to ski.
- Lo so. = I know (it).

6) spedire = to send / mail **(R)**   set 2 -ire

(io) spedisco   (noi) spediamo
(tu) spedisci   (voi) spedite
(lui/lei   spedisce   (loro) spediscono
   Lei)

- Lui spedisce un pacco a casa. = He's sending a package home.
- Spediamo una cartolina. = We're mailing a postcard.
- Spediscila! = Mail it! (Command form - 'tu')

Words + Phrases

- Tanto = Many / Very / A lot

Just like 'molto', 'tanto' can be used as an adjective (many), in which case it agrees with the noun, or an adverb (very / a lot), where it remains unmodified. The main difference between 'molto' and 'tanto' is that 'tanto' is more emphatic.

'Tanto' as an adjective:

→ Ci sono tanti ragazzi. = There are many kids.

'Tanto' as an adverb:

→ Siete tanto gentili. = You all are very nice.

→ Mangio tanto. = I eat a lot.

- Troppo = Too many (adjective) Too much (adverb)

  Same rules apply to 'troppo' as 'tanto.'

→ Lui ha troppi gatti. = He has too many cats.

→ Lei è troppo bella. = She is too beautiful.

→ Dormi troppo. = You sleep too much.

- Tutto = Everything
- Tutti = Everybody
- Tra = Between / Among
- Tu = You (singular and informal)
- Tardi = Late
- Tuo = Your (Possessive pronoun)
- Ti voglio bene = I love you
- Ti amo = I love you

While both phrases mean 'I love you', 'Ti amo' is reserved for that extra special someone.

Tutto a posto.
=
Everything's good (in place).
[In response to
'**Come sta?**'
or
'**Come va?**']

106

T

Words + Phrases

Tuo = Yours (singular you)

→ il tuo cane = your dog   (singular, masculine)
→ i tuoi conigli = your rabbits (plural, masculine)
→ la tua gatta = your (female) cat (singular, feminine)
→ le tue capre = your goats   (plural, feminine)

And for family:

→ tua zia = your aunt
but le tue zie = your aunts

→ tuo zio = your uncle
but i tuoi zii = your uncles or your aunts
                    and uncles

`Zii` is the plural of `zio`. Because the accent falls on the final `i`, you must double them up in the plural.

Remember that the masculine plural form, when describing people, can either mean all guys or a mix of guys and girls.

T

(il) • tempo = a period of time / weather

When 'tempo' refers to time, it indicates a period or quantity.
→ Quanto tempo stai a Roma? = How much time are you staying in Rome?

When 'tempo' refers to weather, use the following phrases:

Che tempo fa? = What's the weather like?

Some responses with 'fa':
→ Fa bello / Fa bel tempo. = It's beautiful out.
→ Fa brutto. Fa brutto tempo. = It's not nice out.
→ Fa caldo. = It's hot.
→ Fa freddo. = It's cold.
→ Fa fresco. = It's cool.

Responses using 'c'è' (there is) and 'ci sono' (there are):
→ C'è il sole. = There's sun.
→ C'è il vento. = There's wind.
→ C'è la nebbia. = There's fog.
→ C'è la neve. = There's snow.
→ C'è la pioggia. = There's rain.
→ Ci sono le nuvole. = There are clouds.

You can also use these 2 verbs:
→ Piove. = It's raining.
→ Nevica. = It's snowing.

Phrases that use 'È' (It's):
• È ventoso. = It's windy.
• È nuvoloso. = It's cloudy.
• È sereno. = It's nice out.
• È afoso. = It's humid.

T

Nouns

(il) • tassì / taxi = taxi

(la) • tavola = table (where you eat)

(il) • tavolo = table (on end table)

(la) • trattoria = a casual restaurant

(il) • tramezzino = crustless sandwich

(il) • tè = caffeinated tea

(la) • tisana = herbal tea

(la) • tazza = mug

(la) • terrazza = terrace
(also, `terrazzo`)

(la) • tenda = curtain

(il) • tuono = thunder

(il) • tetto = roof

(la) • tempesta = storm

(la) • torre = tower

(la) • tabaccheria / tabaccaio = (il)
(An odds and ends shop where
you can purchase gum, candy,
postcards and bus tickets.
Remember to purchase your bus
tickets before you get on the bus!)

(la) • torta = cake

(la) • terra = land

(il) • treno = train

(il) • teatro = theater
(for live performance)

(il) • tramonto = sunset

(la) • taglia = size

(il) • taglio = cut

(la) • tosse = cough

(la) • televisione / tivù = tv
(also, `televisore`)

(il) • telefono = phone

(il) • telefonino = cell phone
(also, `cellulare`)

(il) • tacco = heel (on a shoe)

(il) • tappeto = carpet, rug

(il) • tesoro = treasure

You can call someone
`tesoro` as a term
of endearment
meaning
`darling`

109

1) tornare = to return (R)

(io)	torno	(noi)	torniamo
(tu)	torni	(voi)	tornate
(lui/lei/ Lei)	torna	(loro)	tornano

Used to mean a person is returning, not to return an object.

- Torno a casa alle diciotto. = I'll return home at 6:00pm.
- Tornate a Bari? = Will you all return to Bari?

2) telefonare = to call / telephone (R)

(io)	telefono	(noi)	telefoniamo
(tu)	telefoni	(voi)	telefonate
(lui/lei/ Lei)	telefona	(loro)	telefonano

You can also use 'chiamare' = to call. If using 'telefonare' follow with 'a'.

- Franco telefona a Martina. = Franco is calling Martina.
- Telefoniamo alla mamma. = We're calling Mom.

3) trovare = to find (R)

(io)	_____	(noi)	_____
(tu)	_____	(voi)	_____
(lui/lei/ Lei)	_____	(loro)	_____

Fill in the conjugation yourself!

110

U

Sounds like 'ooh' (even when it begins a word)

Words + Phrases

- utile = useful
- ultimo = last
- uguale = equal
- unico = only, unique

All of these words are adjectives, so their endings will change based on the noun they describe.

Remember the 4 indefinite articles from the beginning of the book? They all begin with 'u'.

Masculine → **un** ristorante
→ **uno** zoo

Feminine → **una** stazione
→ **un'** università

Nouns

- (l') • uccello = bird
- (l') • uomo = man
- (gli) • uomini = men
- (l') • università = university
- (l') • uovo = egg (plural = uova) _le_
- (l') • umore = temperament
- (l') • uscita = exit
- (l') • uva = grapes
- (l') • uvetta = raisin
- (l') • ufficio postale = post office
- (l') • ufficio = office

'essere di buon umore' = to be in a good mood
'essere di cattivo umore' = to be in a bad mood
(conjugate) → Oggi, sono di cattivo umore.
Today, I'm in a bad mood.

U

Verbs

1) uscire = to go out (I)

(io)	esco	(noi)	usciamo
(tu)	esci	(voi)	uscite
(lui/lei Lei)	esce	(loro)	escono

Because it's irregular, most of the conjugations begin with 'e'.

- Esci venerdì sera? = Are you going out Friday evening?
- Usciamo insieme. = We're going out together.

2) usare = to use (R)

(io)	uso	(noi)	usiamo
(tu)	usi	(voi)	usate
(lui/lei Lei)	usa	(loro)	usano

- Uso spesso il mio computer. = I often use my computer.
- Possiamo usare la vostra macchina? = Can we use your car?

Remember, 'potere' and 'dovere' are often conjugated, then followed by an infinitive. See 'V' for the last modal verb.

3) urlare = to yell (R)

Fill in the conjugations yourself!

(io)	_____	(noi)	_____
(tu)	_____	(voi)	_____
(lui/lei Lei)	_____	(loro)	_____

V

Words + Phrases

- Veramente = Really / Truly
- Vicino = Nearby
  → È vicino il museo? = Is the museum nearby?
- Voi = You all (subject pronoun)
- Vietato = Prohibited
- Vietato entrare = Do not enter
- Vietato fumare = No smoking

(You'll see 'vietato' on signs telling you not to do certain things).

- Vostro = Yours - plural you (Possessive pronoun, see below.)
- Vieni qui = Come here

Vorrei..
=
I would like..

(A polite way to request something. Use in ordering food and in stores.)

→ **Vorrei un caffè**
=
I would like a coffee.

Vostro

'Vostro' means yours, but refers to something(s) belonging to 2 or more people.

- il vostro cuscino = your pillow   (singular, masculine)
- i vostri coperti = your blankets   (plural, masculine)
- la vostra lampada = your lamp   (singular, feminine)
- le vostre poltrone = your armchairs   (plural, feminine)

E per la famiglia:

→ vostra nipote = your niece / granddaughter
  but le vostre nipoti

→ vostro nipote = your nephew / grandson
  but i vostri nipoti

'Nipote' has 4 different meanings! The context and article / possessive pronoun will make the meaning clear.

113

V

(il) • volo = flight/plane

(il) • vitello = veal (eaten more commonly in Italy)

(la) • villa = country house

(la) • vacanza = vacation

(la) • voglia = desire

(la) • vita = life

(la) • via = street

(il) • viale = avenue

(il) • vetro = glass

(la) • verità = truth

(il) • vicino = neighbor

(la) • volta = time

(il) • vaticano = where the Pope lives. (Vatican City is an independent state).

(il) • viso = face

(il) • viaggio = big trip

(la) • valigia = suitcase

(il) • vizio = vice (e.g. smoking)

(il) • venerdì = Friday

(il) • vino = wine

(il) • vulcano = volcano

(la) • vongola = clam

(la) • vacca = cow (You can also say 'mucca').

We've seen that 'Ora' is used for telling time, and 'tempo' describes a period of time. 'Volta' describes time in terms of occurrence:

→ una volta = one time

→ ogni volta = each time

→ due volte = two times plural

→ dieci volte = ten times plural

• Verdura = vegetable

Some common vegetables:

(la) • melanzana = eggplant

(l') • aglio = garlic

(la) • cipolla = onion

(i) • broccoli = broccoli

(il) • pomodoro = tomato

(il) • basilico = basil

(il) • peperone = bell pepper

(la) • carota = carrot

(lo) • zucchino = squash

(il) • fungo = mushroom

(gli) • spinaci = spinach

(la) • patata = potato

V

Verbs

See letter 'A' for more on 'andare' and 'a', letter 'I' for 'in', and letter 'D' for 'da'.

1) andare = to go (I)

(io) vado	(noi) andiamo
(tu) vai	(voi) andate
(lui/lei va Lei)	(loro) vanno

Follow any conjugation of 'andare' with **'a'** + an **infinitive verb** when going to go do another activity:

→ Vado **a** mangiare. = I'm going to eat.
→ Andiamo **a** ballare. = We're going to dance.

Follow with **'a'** as an **articulated preposition** (see grammar section) when going to most places:

→ Vai **al** supermercato. = You're going to the supermarket.
→ Andate **alla** farmacia. = You all are going to the pharmacy.

Follow with **'a'** unmodified for the following places:

- casa = home
- scuola = school
- teatro = theater
- with all cities

→ Lui va **a** casa. = He's going home.
→ Vanno **a** Firenze. = They're going to Florence.

Follow with **'in'** unmodified for these places:

- chiesa = church
- biblioteca = library
- campagna = countryside
- ufficio = office
- centro = downtown
- montagna = mountains
- vacanza = vacation
- with all countries, regions

→ Lei va **in** montagna. = She's/you're (formal) going to the mountains.
→ Vado **in** Toscana. = I'm going to Tuscany.

Follow with **'da'** (sometimes articulated) when going to someone's house or place of business:

→ Vai **da** Giorgio. = You're going to Giorgio's house.
→ Lui va **dal** medico. = He's going to the doctor.

115

Verbs

2) volere = to want (I)

(io) voglio   (noi) vogliamo
(tu) vuoi   (voi) volete
(lui/lei / Lei) vuole   (loro) vogliono

'Volere' is the last of the modal verbs. It follows the same rules as the two we've already seen, 'dovere' and 'potere'. All of these modal verbs when followed by another verb, will be conjugated. The verb to follow will be left in the infinitive.

• Voglio viaggiare quest'estate. = I want to travel this summer.

'Questo/a' can be shortened to quest' in front of a vowel.

• Volete pranzare insieme? = Do you all want to eat lunch together?

• Vogliono una nuova macchina. = They want a new car.

You can, of course, follow the verb with a noun.

Use the polite form of 'volere' (the conditional) when making a request.

(io) vorrei = I would like
(tu) vorresti = You would like
(lui/lei) (Lei) vorrebbe → He/she would like → You (formal) would like

(noi) vorremmo = We would like
(voi) vorreste = You all would like
(loro) vorrebbero = They would like

• Vorrei un caffè per favore. = I would like a coffee please.

116

Verbs

3) venire = to come (I)

(io) vengo   (noi) veniamo
(tu) vieni   (voi) venite
(lui/lei viene   (loro) vengono
    Lei)

Review 'disjunctive pronouns.'

- Vieni con me? = Are you coming with me?
- Possiamo venire alla vostra festa. = We can come to your party.
- Venga! = Come here! **(F)** – command

4) visitare = to visit (R)

(io) visito   (noi) visitiamo
(tu) visiti   (voi) visitate
(lui/lei visita   (loro) visitano
    Lei)

- Visitano il museo. = They're visiting the museum.
- Visito molti bei paesi. = I'll visit many beautiful countries.

The phrase **'andare a trovare'** is used more commonly than 'visitare' to express going to visit someone.

→ Vado a trovare la mia amica. = I'm going to visit my friend.

'Viaggiare' = to travel **(R)**

See if you can conjugate on your own →

io _____   noi _____
tu _____   voi _____
lui/lei _____   loro _____
Lei

Verbs

5) **vedere** = to see (R)

(io)	vedo	(noi)	vediamo
(tu)	vedi	(voi)	vedete
(lui/lei Lei)	vede	(loro)	vedono

- Lei vede l'orario? = Do you (formal) see the schedule?
- Ci vediamo domani. = We'll see each other tomorrow.
  (reciprocal / reflexive)
- Non vedo l'ora di partire. = I can't wait to leave.
  (An idiomatic phrase ～→ 'Non vedo l'ora' = I can't wait)

The words 'arrivederci / arrivederla' contain 4 different elements!

a = until
ri = again
veder = to see
  ci = each other
or la = you (formal)

Succinctly say 'arrivederci' or 'arrivederla' (in formal situations), to mean, 'until we see each other again'.

conjugate
↙ yourself!

6) **vivere** = to live (R)

'Abitare' also means 'to live' but is specific to a dwelling or place. 'vivere' can also refer to a dwelling or place, as well as living in a general sense.

(io)	_____	(noi)	_____
(tu)	_____	(voi)	_____
(lui/lei Lei)	_____	(loro)	_____

- Vivi in Francia? = Do you live in France?
- Viviamo bene. = We live well.

Z

The 'z' sound is either

'dz' → when beginning a word

or

'ts' → in the middle of a word

Contrast the sound of the 'z' in these words:

- Zona = dz·oh·nah
- pizza = pee·ts·ah

Remember that the 's', when in between 2 vowels, sounds like a 'z' in English. eg. → Pisa = (Pee·zah)

Nouns

(lo) • zoo = zoo
(Remember the 'oo' is pronounced like 'oh').

(la) • zona = area

(la) • zuppa = soup

(la) • zucca = pumpkin

(la) • zanzara = mosquito

(la) • zia = aunt

(lo) • zio = uncle

(lo) • zaino = backpack

     (gli)   (le)
• zucchini / zucchine
=
squash

Index

buono (good), 21, 39
(to) buy, 48
   by, 25, 34, 65

C

caffè (coffee), 44, 75, 76
caldo (hot), 36, 56, 108
(to) call, 46, 110
(to) call oneself, 10
capire (to understand), 47
(to) carry, bring, wear, 93
c'è, ci sono (there is, are), 43, 108
cenare (to have dinner), 48
cercare (to look for), 6, 46
che (what, how), 42, 43, 56
-82, 108
chi (who), 42
chiamare (to call), 46
chiamarsi (to call oneself)
-10, 42
city vocabulary, 50, 76
clothing, 67
coffee, 44, 75, 76
colazione (breakfast), 40, 55
cold, 36, 56, 108
colors, 18
come (how), 42
(to) come, 117
cominciare, (to begin), 48
commands
    regular, 12
    irregular, 13

comprare (to buy), 48
con (with), 25, 33
conoscere (to know), 47
conto (bill), 46
cosa (what), 42

D

da (from, to), 25, 49, 115
(to) dance, 41
definite articles, 22, 23
   with possessive pronouns
   -27, 69, 73, 78, 100, 107, 113
(to) depart, 92
desiderare (to desire), 52
desire, 36, 116
di (of, from), 25, 49, 51
dire (to say, tell), 52
direct object pronouns,
-28, 29
directions, 50, 63
disjunctive pronouns, 33
divertirsi (to have fun), 10
(to) do, make, 55
dormire (to sleep), 8
dove (where), 49, 50
dovere (to have to), 51
(to) dress oneself, 10
(to) drink, 41

E

(to) eat, 74
ecco (here), 29, 53
(to) enjoy oneself, 10
-ere verbs, 7
essere (to be), 54, 103, 104
  with time, 82-84
excuse me, 86, 98
(to) exercise, 55
expressions of time, 65, 99
expressions
  with avere, 36
  with fare, 55

F

fa (ago), 99
fame (hunger), 36
family, 69, 73, 78, 100, 107, 113
far away, 68
fare (to do, make), 55
  expressions with, 55
  bodily pain, 56
  weather, 56, 108
fear, 36
(to) feel, 102
feminine
  adjectives, 18-21, 24
  nouns, 14-16
fermarsi (to stop), 10
feste (holidays), 60
(to) find, 110
finire (to finish), 9, 58
(to) finish, 9, 58
food, 74-76

for, 25
formal, 1, 2
fra (between, among), 25, 58
freddo (cold), 36, 56, 108
frequentare (to attend), 58
fretta (haste), 36
from, 25, 26, 49, 51
fruit, 59
frutta (fruit), 59

G

gender
  adjectives, 18-21, 24
  nouns, 14-16
(to) get up, 10, 102
giocare (to play), 63
girare (to turn), 63
(to) give, 52
(to) go, 36, 115
(to) go out, 112
good bye, 34, 39, 42, 98, 118
grazie (thank you), 62, 72
guardare (to watch), 63

H

haste, 36
(to) have, 36, 64
(to) have to, 51
(to) have dinner, 48
health, 56, 57
(to) hear, 102
hello, 39, 42, 98

124